The People Project Triangle

The People Project Triangle

Balancing Delivery, Business-as-Usual, and People's Welfare

Stuart Copeland and Andy Coaton

BEP BUSINESS EXPERT PRESS

First published in 2020 by
Business Expert Press, LLC
222 East 46th Street, New York, NY 10017
www.businessexpertpress.com

ISBN-13: 978-1-95152-760-0 (paperback)
ISBN-13: 978-1-95152-761-7 (e-book)

Business Expert Press Portfolio and Project Management Collection

Collection ISSN: 2156-8189 (print)
Collection ISSN: 2156-8200 (electronic)

Cover and interior design by Exeter Premedia Services Private Ltd., Chennai, India

First edition: 2020

10 9 8 7 6 5 4 3 2 1

Printed in the United States of America.

Abstract

The modern business environment is one of rapid change. The modern corporation is lean and very cost conscious. A consequence is an increasingly common project management situation of a medium important, medium complex business change project that cannot justify a full-time team. It is, therefore, largely staffed by in-house resources working on the project as *homework*, that is, in addition to their normal responsibilities. We term this a *composite* project.

The thesis of the book is that composite projects are being used at an increasing rate to meet the demands of rapid business change. However, they are largely unrecognized as a separate organizational category of project, with particular characteristics, management needs, and risks.

Analogous to the classic project *Iron Triangle*, where there is a trade-off between cost, time and scope, we maintain that there is a People Project Triangle. This is a trade-off between the project, the ongoing business, and the people working in both the business and the project. When pressure mounts, generally, only two of those can be prioritized, and one must give. We observe that it is often the people who bear the brunt with subsequent implications of stress and burnout.

Drawing on our experience, we assert that, with better recognition, clearer understanding and appropriate measures, many of the common problems with composite projects can be foreseen and avoided or mitigated.

Keywords

Project management; programme management; program management; business change; projects as homework; stakeholder management; workplace stress; composite project; project resourcing; project team; project leadership; project sponsor; business lead

Contents

Prologue

If the story that follows has any resonance for you, if you recognize something of your organization, if you often share the anguish and frustration of these characters, then this is the book for you.

Project Kark Rash

Matt Mefford, a project manager at Nat Retail Brands Limited (NRB) and responsible for the new Training Center operational launch, again looked anxiously at his watch. In less than an hour, he would have to face Malcolm Shots, the CEO, and he had no idea what he was going to tell him.

They had launched on time, but it was a seriously cut back launch and certainly did not have the *wow factor* the CEO had wanted. The first delegate survey was terrible. Also, he looked again at the project finance report telling him he was 10 percent over budget. He knew the Marketing Director had already blamed pressure from his project for the delay in delivering the quarterly marketing reports. And, two of the project team went onto sick leave the day after opening, leaving the operation under massive pressure from Day One.

He also suspected one of his project team, who happened to know Malcolm socially from the golf club, had been bad mouthing him for *acting like a dictator*.

He just could not understand what had gone wrong. He had followed the company's project management method to the letter, but the damned project team members just kept coming up with excuses and he just could not get them to pull their fingers out and get on with it.

Matt

Matt Mefford began his career in an IT department as a Business Analyst and later become a Project Manager gaining his PRINCE2 accreditation.

He had run increasingly larger projects, initially in IT and later across other business areas and sectors. He was regarded as an experienced PM with a strong track record.

The New Training Center

Employing 250 at the head office and 15,000 operational staff, NRB was a national retailer with 300 sites around the country. Historically, staff were trained locally in the regions, but it was thought more effective to bring it all together into a single training center known as the STC. Large savings in external accommodation costs were expected, as well as establishing a center of excellence to act as a showcase for the company.

The Facilities team proceeded with the project of organizing the physical build of the training center and hotel. This ran to schedule thanks to the hard work of the Facilities team and their selection of an excellent prime contractor.

First Steps

At a routine monthly planning meeting, the CEO noticed the STC launch was due in six months, "Sally, what plans do you have to open this new facility?" he asked the operations director. "We've got six months to sort the internal fit out, the business processes, recruit the team and so on."

"I'll get onto it," responded Sally.

"OK, Sally, this is a prestige launch. I don't need to remind you it's critical we have a smooth opening."

Setting up the Project

Sally Opsdee had been running the Operations Division for five years, knew the business well, and had plenty of experience making successful changes within her division.

The next day, Sally met with Bob Bild, the Facilities Director. Sally and Bob had a good working relationship and often collaborated on projects. "I need a PM to get us over the line on this one. I've heard Matt gets things done."

"When it comes to delivery, he doesn't take any prisoners," agreed Bob. "And he covers my back on audit, compliance and so on." Satisfied, Sally pressed on, "I want to email out today, so we can crack on. I'll obviously go to their managers first, but what do you think of these other people for the team? I'm thinking Linda, Jim, Mo, Rashid, Sid and Jo?"

"Yes, that's all the 'go to' people. They're the experts," Bob added, "You might want to check they're free."

"No problem," replied Sally. "I'm sure they can fit it in, great group of people."

A couple of days later, Sally met with Matt. "This is a great chance to show your prowess as a deliverer. I've put together a brief outlining what we expect on opening." Smiling she handed over a loose, half-page brief. "We really want to wow the delegates and set an example for how things should be done."

Matt was a bit uncomfortable with the low level of detail, but this was his first project with Sally, and he did not want to come across as difficult. So, he let it go.

Planning the Project

Matt quickly organized an all-day workshop for the team to flesh out Sally's limited brief. Enthusiasm for the new training center was high, and everyone turned up, keen to make an input.

"Thanks everyone for your attendance today," opened Matt. He then covered the background to the project and the brief. "We need your help today to turn that outline brief into a project plan and flush out risks, assumptions and dependencies."

Matt expertly guided the project team through a product-based planning session creating the product breakdown structure, covering all the deliverables. From this, the group was able to assess dependencies, identify assumptions, and document their risks and some high-level mitigation.

Afterward, the team was chatting over a cup of tea.

"I was impressed by Matt's approach," offered Linda. "Starting from what we need for go live, then planning backwards. The rest was a bit dull, but I see why we needed to do it."

Jim was less comfortable, "Do you realize how much work this will be. Sally's email didn't make that clear. Another project done as homework."

Rashid had worked with Matt before. "And Matt will make sure the project gets delivered so don't expect an easy ride."

"I think we've seen that already—two-hour weekly review meetings plus one-hour one-to-ones have already gone into my diary. I hope he realizes I've got a full-time job already," Jo's eyes turned skyward.

"Yes," said Mo, "and they run through with no gaps for month end."

Unaware of the tentative concern in the team, Matt was happy with his day's work. He could now build a plan, assign resources, and provide people with their task lists.

Matt also wanted to make sure he had sign off from the business stakeholders so, once completed, he e-mailed a detailed plan and RAID log. The instruction was to review and sign off by the end of the week. Matt said he would assume sign off if he had not heard back by then.

He had his sponsor and weekly meetings with her, his team, his plan, and signoff, so he could crack on!

Running the Project

Six weeks later and Matt was starting to become anxious. He was with Sally in their weekly meeting. "I thought everyone had agreed the plan, but they're always late on tasks, never complete their reports on time and miss loads of meetings."

Sally was concerned. "This doesn't sound like a 'green' project, Matt. I don't want to scare the senior guys, but we do need to get on top of this."

Sally leaned forward in her chair, "Well, Matt, it's your job to sort it out. This project is just as important as anything else in the business right now. I'll back you up."

Emboldened by Sally, Matt became more assertive. He insisted on attendance at all meetings with the threat of escalation to line managers. Attendance improved, but Matt started to notice a certain coldness and abruptness in conversions with the team, and tasks were still not getting done.

Matt decided he needed to *have it out* with the team. The plan review in the next meeting was conducted more rigorously and the team responded in kind. "I appreciate this is important but it's not in my objectives." "These meetings clash with the month end process." "I do have a day job, you know."

However, to his relief, the team did respond, and the project started to draw back to plan.

Back on Track, Sort Of

At the 12-week meeting with Sally, Matt was able to report the plan was nearly back on track. Unfortunately, Sally had to tell him she had had a series of complaints from the operational managers that the normal working of departments was being badly affected by the project.

Matt was starting to feel the pressure. "I'm between a rock and a hard place, I can't win." He pushed more pressure on the project team to deliver their project tasks. Further resentment built up among some of the team members. Given there are only so many hours in the day, some chose to prioritize the project, some chose to prioritize their business-as-usual activity, and some worked extra hours to do both.

On the run-up to opening, Matt proposed, and Sally very reluctantly agreed to delay some non-essential items till after opening. The project was behind schedule, and the opening day could not be moved. The complaints from the operational managers continued about how much time was being devoted to the project. And, two of the team had complained to HR about their workload and their concerns were being ignored.

Matt and the team had enough of a relationship to get the project across the line. It was not pretty, which frustrated Matt. It seemed less of a concern to the project team who were used to operational emergencies. However, the project had left a trail of minor chaos behind it. No one in the business was happy; there was a significant follow-on task list, and two of the project team members were signed off with stress.

Opening Day

Opening day arrived and the facility was in good shape. However, the arrival process for delegates was shambolic, and some of the internal fit-out had not been thought through. The Delegate Experience Survey was the worst ever recorded on an NRB training course. The budget was over-spent by 10 percent. The project manager and the project team were an unhappy bunch and the operations director was disappointed. All their reputations had been affected, and it was a very tired group of people.

Meeting the CEO

Standing outside the CEO's office, Matt paused before knocking on the door. It was a cold day, but he felt a bead of sweat run down the back of his neck. He was not looking forward to this meeting.

What was the key issue that Matt faced but never actually recognized? What did he get right, and where could he have done better?

Acknowledgment

We would like to thank the people who have contributed to our ideas on this topic. To all our colleagues and clients on projects. But especially to John Niland and Andy Bray. John suggested to Stuart, over a lunch at St Pancras International Rail Station, that he should start a book. Andy Bray who has been making a living for 15 years managing composite projects and as guest lecturer on one of the author's MSc programs patiently discusses these issues with his students each year.

We are profoundly grateful to the small team who volunteered to critique, challenge, and try to understand the book. A big thanks to Mike Churchman, John Eary, Alex Coaton, Hannah Rogers, and Fiona Copeland.

Finally, we want to acknowledge the support of our families, particularly our wives, Fiona and Sally, for their encouragement and tolerance. It turns out writing a book is hard and takes a lot of time.

Stuart Copeland and Andy Coaton,
Milton Keynes, United Kingdom
January 2020

CHAPTER 1

Introduction

Aim of the Book

This is a book about business projects. Projects that aim to change the way business-as-usual (BaU) is done. Projects that happen every day in all industries and functional areas. Medium-important, medium-complex, business change projects. Projects like the one in the previous story, projects such as relocating facilities, introducing new computer systems, re-engineering departments around processes, or adapting to new regulations.

Pressures on the modern business environment have resulted in lean and very cost-conscious modern organizations. A consequence is these types of medium-important business projects are unable to justify a full-time team. Instead, they are largely staffed by in-house resources working on the project, in addition to their normal responsibilities.

The thesis of the book is that this form of project structure is being used at an increasing rate to meet the demands of rapid business change. However, they are largely unrecognized as a separate organizational category of project, with particular characteristics, management needs, and risks. The consequence is not only project failures, but staff with damaged reputations or who are burned out.

We offer solutions.

It is not an academic tome. It is a practical business book advocating a particular approach for a particular type of project. It is born of observation from the extensive experience of project management practitioners. That experience is as in-house project managers, external project managers, and business consultancy project managers over a period of 30 years across a range of sectors.

Who can benefit from this book? Our target audience is:

- People who initiate projects.
- People who sponsor projects.
- People who lead projects and who want to make the shift from the competent method-driven practitioner to a highly effective stakeholder-focused professional.

The approach advocated by this book is compatible with project methodologies PRINCE2, Association for Project Management (APM), and Project Management Institute (PMI), and also the principles behind Agile. We have largely assumed the reader is familiar with one or more of these standards. The approach described in this book should be used to help tailor your methodology for this specific category of project.

Project Categorization

The project categorization used in this book is shown in Figure 1.1. It distinguishes three types of projects dependent on how they are organized and staffed. This is not a conventional categorization, but one we hope you will recognize and, most importantly, allow us to identify a neglected aspect of managing projects in the modern corporation.

The first type are the most complex projects. They are strategic, major cross-company or inter-company (supply chain) business transformations. Examples include major systems introduction such an Enterprise Resource Planning (ERP) system, introduction of just-in-time processes, culture change such as moving the organization to customer focused, or strategic reorientations such as moving major revenue earning to services and away from product sales.

These projects have a full project management structure and are staffed with professional project teams dedicated to the project. We will refer to these as Level 1 strategic projects.

At the other end of the scale, the least business complex projects are conducted within the existing BaU structures. Examples include projects that deliver tactical outputs such a building refurbishment, department information technology (IT) projects, process improvements, and

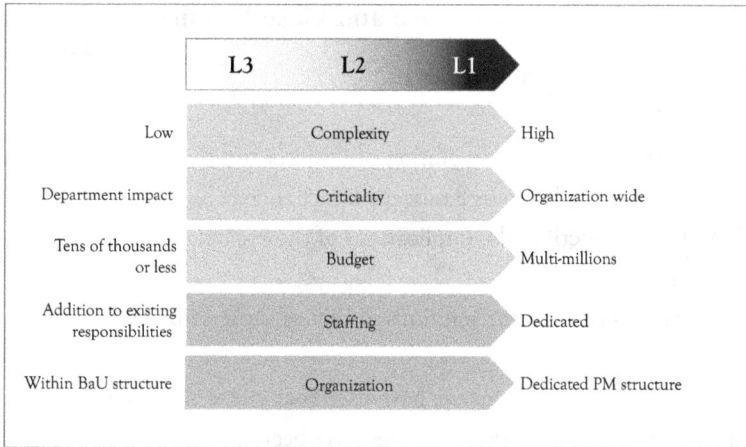

	L3	L2	L1	
Low		Complexity		High
Department impact		Criticality		Organization wide
Tens of thousands or less		Budget		Multi-millions
Addition to existing responsibilities		Staffing		Dedicated
Within BaU structure		Organization		Dedicated PM structure

Figure 1.1 Categorizing projects

Source: Images from http://clipart-library.com

intra-departmental organizational change. The team is almost always drawn from the permanent staff who will lead, manage, and support the project as part of their existing responsibilities. The project will not be of a scale to significantly disrupt their workload or BaU. We will refer to these as Level 3 tactical projects.

There is a remaining category. Projects that are too large a scale and too complex to be run within the BaU structures, but do not warrant a fully dedicated project team. Examples might be large-scale interlinked outputs such as facility relocation, new computer systems, process re-engineering, or cross-company reorganization. To staff these projects, dedicated full-time project resources are supported with business leadership and expertise from the permanent staff. As the staffing is a blend of staff dedicated to the project and staff part-time on the project, we will refer to these as Level 2 projects or *composite* projects.

In our experience, Level 3 and Level 1 projects are well understood by organizations and, on the whole, managed well, delivering desired outcomes within controlled budget and timescales. However, we regularly see Level 2 composite projects fail to deliver as expected. We believe this is because they are not recognized for what they are and so are not organized and managed optimally. This book is focused on these Level 2 composite projects: how to recognize them, understand common failings of them, and how to best manage them.

Book Structure and Case Studies

This book is written in three parts:

- Part I describes the evolution of projects and their management as the business landscape has changed.
- Part II describes the implications of those changes on business and their staff.
- Part III offers some solutions to reduce those impacts.

To illustrate our points, we have used many case studies drawn from real projects we have worked on. They have been rendered anonymous for two reasons: to meet obligations under non-disclosure agreements and we do not wish to embarrass or offend.

PART I

The Changing Project Environment

CHAPTER 2

The Why and How
of Projects

Organizations: The Why?

Most of us spend a lot of our time in organizations. They exist because, to achieve anything of any size and complexity, many people need to work together. Over time, organizations, including corporations, have become bigger and more complex, to achieve bigger and more complex impacts on the world.

The purposes of organizations fall into broad categories. The purpose of a government may be to enable the people of a nation to live in safety and happiness. A charity's purpose may be the advancement of animal welfare, and a corporation's purpose is probably the maximization of shareholder value.

To advance their purpose, an organization strives to achieve its mission. India's National Council for Civil Liberties strives to "Fight Injustice and to Attack Evils" and Google strives "to organize the world's information and make it universally accessible and useful."

To deliver on their mission, an organization has strategic goals. The Institute of Cancer Research has a goal to make an "impact on survival rates, duration of remission and alleviation of side effects of cancer treatment." Corporations have the goal of increasing profit year on year.

Organizations: The How

The role of projects in organizations is shown in Figure 2.1. To achieve a goal requires a strategy. A corporation with a goal of growing profit in the

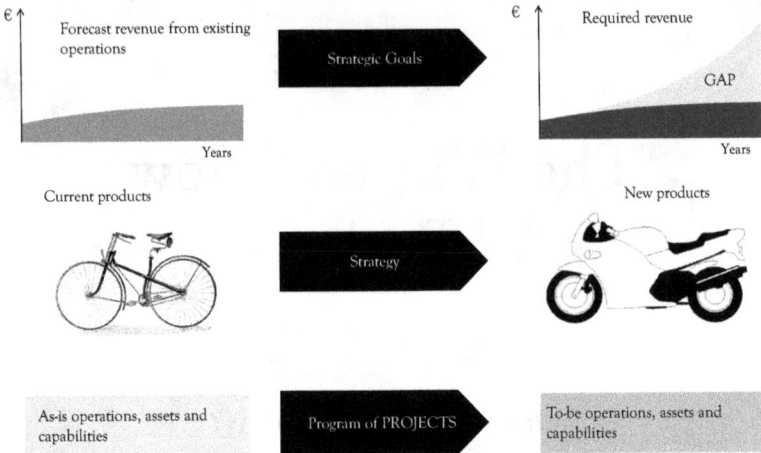

Figure 2.1 How organizations remain competitive

face of competition may have a strategy of cost leadership or quality leadership; it may try to do more of the same better or deliver new products to existing customers or the same products to new customers. But, whatever the strategy, it will require transforming the existing operations, assets, and capabilities into a different set of operations, assets, and capabilities. To bring about this transformation, an organization uses a program of projects.

So, it is clear for an organization to survive and prosper, it must be able to effectively run projects that deliver on required outcomes to enhance its operations, assets, and capabilities.

How Are Projects Different from Business-as-Usual (BaU)?

This book is about managing projects, so it is important we are clear what makes something a project. How is it different from business-as-usual (BaU)? The box provides the definition of a project given by PRINCE2. The other bodies give slightly different definitions but are essentially similar.

A Project

PRINCE2 defines a project as "a temporary organization that is created for the purpose of delivering one or more business products according to an agreed Business Case."

For example, the business product could be a new building, an upgraded computer system, or a staff reorganization.

The definition captures some key features that makes something a project:

- Finite duration
- Specific deliverables
- The deliverables will provide agreed benefits
- Defined scope
- Unique and one-off
- Uncertain and risky
- And, usually multi-disciplined and cross-functional or cross-enterprise with complex relationships

Business as Usual (BaU)

This is the ongoing operations of the organization. The people, processes, systems, and facilities used to create and deliver the services and products to meet the needs of the organization's customers.

BaU is the ongoing operations of the business. All the things the organization does to satisfy customer demand. The persistent consistent provision of goods and services that earns the organization its income.

In contrast to BaU, which is expected to continue indefinitely, a project has *finite duration*, which means there is a start and most importantly an end date. A project has *specific deliverables* (in PRINCE2 terminology, products), that is, it creates some things or changes some things. Deliverables might be physical objects like buildings or software systems, or it

Table 2.1 Projects versus BaU

Feature	BaU Management	Project Management
Responsibility	For status-quo	For change
Authority	Defined by organizational structure	Fuzzy
Tasks	Consistent	Ever-changing
Stability	Permanent	Temporary
Focus	Efficiency	Conflict resolution and trade-offs

might be an outcome like a revised business process, new capabilities, or a trained workforce in place. When the change has happened, then BaU resumes in a new better form.

The deliverables are created to provide *specific benefits*. This is the agreed business case in the PRINCE2 definition. To start a project, there must be a justifiable reason. What is more, it remains justified throughout. The justification is that the agreed benefits exceed the costs.

Table 2.1 summarizes the differences between project management and BaU management. BaU is designed to efficiently produce the same output within defined tolerances. By contrast, projects produce *unique outputs*. Even if an organization does many projects, there will be different outcomes, teams, customers, locations, and other factors. This uniqueness is inherently risky. Almost by definition, if you have not done something before, you will be unsure what will happen. Managing this uncertainty is a key issue in project management. The uncertainty is magnified by the complex relationships created when a cross-functional and multi-disciplined group of people with different perspectives and who do not know each other are working together.

What Is a Program of Projects?

Implementing a strategy usually needs a series of related projects. The management and coordination of these related projects is known as program management. For example, if the strategy is a new service operation in a new market, there may be three coordinated projects to deliver a building, a computer system, and new organizational structure.

A Program of Projects

"Managing Successful Programmes" (MSP) defines a program as "a temporary, flexible organization created to coordinate, direct and oversee the implementation of a set of related projects and activities to deliver outcomes and benefits related to the organization's strategic objectives."

In the last 30 years, program and project management has evolved from a skill confined to information technology (IT) and engineering, particularly construction, to a profession that is recognized across all sectors and functional areas. There are defined and globally recognized methodologies, properly accredited qualifications, and many skilled practitioners.

CHAPTER 3

The Changed Business Landscape

How It Was

If one of today's graduates was taken back in time to the corporate office of the early 1980s, they would notice a few differences. Staff smoked at their desk, and there was no need for *offering to make the tea* etiquette as tea ladies brought mid-morning refreshments around. It was a strict nine to five culture, with the office deserted within 10 minutes of 5 p.m. Sending a memo involved having it typed by a secretary, of which there were many, along with other admin staff. This level of resource was necessary because there were few computers and they were mainframes, off in a distant site somewhere. The new graduate might also be struck by who else was around. Many people worked for the same company all their careers, and they largely felt secure in their jobs. One of the authors remembers his first graduate job at an engineering company in a diversified conglomerate. One of the people he was introduced to was Dan, comfortable at his desk by the window that he seemed to look out most of his day. Dan had been with the company for as long as anyone remembered. When he asked what Dan did, he was told he looked after the s300 range. When he asked whether they still made the s300 range, he was told no, but "there are still quite a few out there and we sometimes get people calling up asking how to calibrate them, or for parts."

The lack of technology would perhaps be the first thing our time-traveling graduate would notice, but, after reflection, they may think that the most profound is that there are no Dans anymore.

In the distant days of the 1980s, people were in the office for 40 hours and had jobs they could comfortably get done in 40 hours. There was also

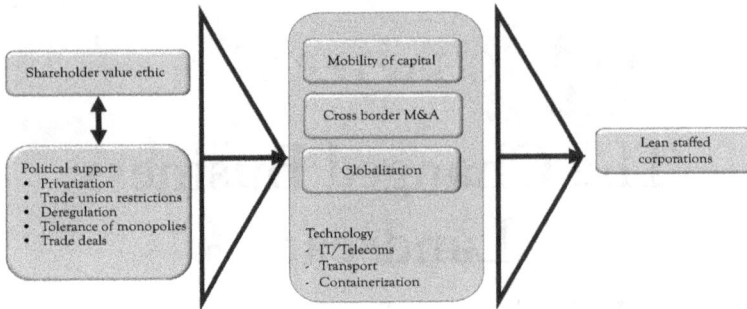

Figure 3.1 Drivers of business change

plenty of people making their way on the management track being moved around from line jobs to overseas posts and back again to head office jobs. And often, they were between roles and available to run a project, maybe introduce one of those new whizzy computer systems, for instance.

It was a comfortable world of short commutes to 40-hour weeks for 40 years, leading to a pension of forty-sixtieths of your final salary. It is a different world now, why did it change? Figure 3.1 lays out the process.

Drivers of Change

The 1980s saw the emergence of several drivers that changed the culture and conditions of the corporate office.

New Business and Political Ethic

Corporations have always been keen on profit of course, but this was seen in a context of a wider societal role. During the 1980s, a new ethic arose in the business schools and board rooms, the ethic of shareholder value. It became to be seen that the only fiduciary duty of the board was to add value for shareholders. At the political level, this was seen as socially desirable because by pursuing this objective, the business would flourish, leading to more wealth to the benefit of society at large.

This ethic was supported by government in many ways, including privatizing nationalized industries and eliminating trade union power, but, possibly, most importantly, in the form of financial deregulation and by taking a permissive attitude to corporate takeovers. In the United States,

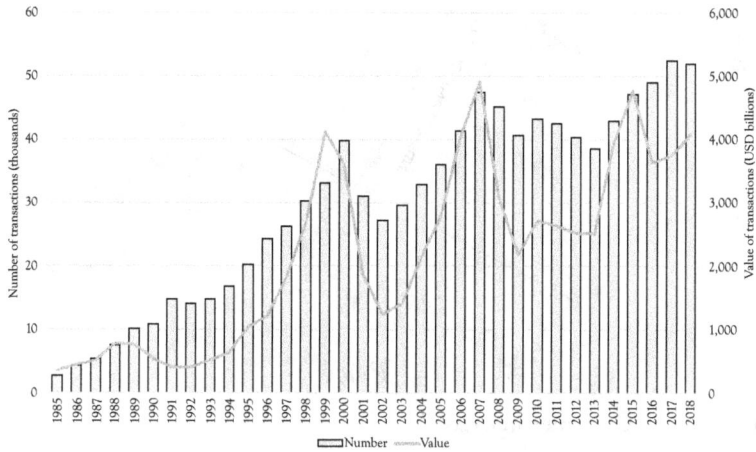

Figure 3.2 Announced mergers and acquisitions worldwide

Source: IMAA Institute, https://imaa-institute.org/mergers-and-acquisitions-statistics/

the antitrust policy and enforcement declined due to the Reagan administration's enforcement priorities, judicial appointments, and submissions to the Supreme Court. In the United Kingdom, the body responsible for making sure companies did not acquire monopoly power, the Monopolies and Mergers Commission symbolically even dropped reference to monopoly and rebranded as the Competition Commission. Corporations are driven to merge and takeover competitors to increase competitiveness, via economies of scale, and increase profits and power by sheer size. The combination of more potential targets and lots of new deregulated banking money led to a large increase in corporate takeover activity (see the preceding chart in Figure 3.2). Increased mergers and acquisitions (M&As) meant that corporate executives not only faced competitive pressure for their products, but also pressure over ownership of their companies. They needed to make their companies fit enough to fight off hostile takeovers or to engage in hostile takeovers.

Business competes by providing products and services. Figure 3.3 is the customer matrix showing the market from the customer's perspective. The diagonal line shows viable competitive strategies in the market. Bottom left sell cheap and cheerful and a low price; top right sell premium high quality for a premium price. But wherever a company is on the line, over time, customers will always be looking for better products at lower

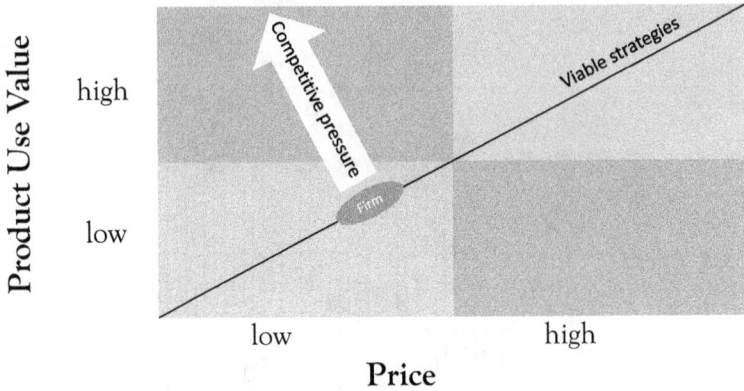

Figure 3.3 Customer matrix

prices. Competitors will be trying to provide them. It is a cliché because it is true: a business must run just to stay still. The pressure is to move the viable strategy line up and left. How is that done?

What does running look like? A business cannot act directly on the consumer matrix; instead, it must act on the producer matrix, see Figure 3.4. It shows the competitive world from the perspective of businesses. To provide products and services with more use value, it must be more effective, that is, provide things that customers value. The price a business can charge is dictated by the unit costs of providing the product or service. In other words, being more efficient allows the business to offer lower prices or make more profit at the same price. To move on the consumer matrix,

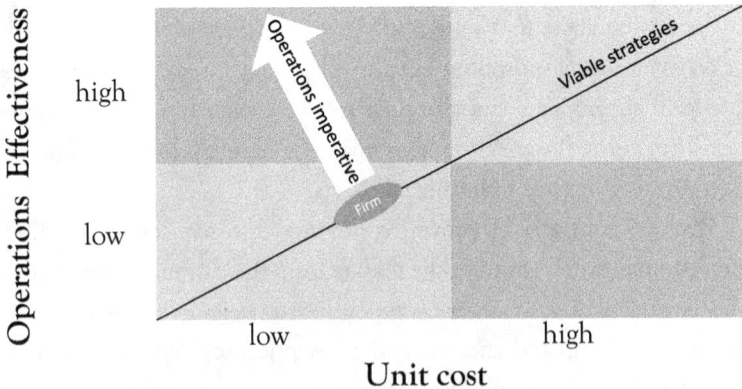

Figure 3.4 Producer matrix

the business must move on the producer matrix up and left. The pressure is for ever-more efficiency. Add value by doing the same with lower costs.

For many businesses, a major cost is people, and so, the major pressure has been to add shareholder value by reducing the size of the workforce.

Globalization

Globalization is the trend of increasing interaction and trade between people and companies on a worldwide scale. It is another major trend and supported by political developments.

The first is the growth of global trading blocs such as the European Union, North American Free Trade Agreement (NAFTA), and Association of Southeast Asian Nations (ASEAN). Within these blocks, there is frictionless trading across national borders because of common regulations and zero tariffs.

The World Trade Organization was formed in 1995. It establishes frameworks for international trade, facilitating trade deals between countries and trading blocs, resulting in reduced tariff and other barriers.

Financial deregulation, mentioned earlier, has meant a general reduction in legal barriers to the movement of capital, making it easier for capital to flow between different economies. This means firms can finance expansion into foreign markets and engineer profits to be made in low tax jurisdictions.

There has been increased mobility of labor. Although still a small percentage of the global population, according to UN[1] Migration Reports, in 2017, 258 million people lived outside their countries of origin, up by 100 million since 1990. It is not always optimal for corporations to site assets in countries with the lowest cost labor. Sometimes, it is best to import the labor to existing assets. This might be cheap labor to pick peaches in South Carolina or pick Amazon orders in warehouses in Texas, or it might be the highly educated for tech companies in Silicon Valley. Corporations have wanted it, so governments have facilitated widespread immigration. Given this pull from corporations in the West, citizens of

---

[1] International Migration Reports, 2013 and 2017. United Nations, Department of Economic and Social Affairs

developing countries have responded to the chance to improve their economic prospects. The unskilled, but also the educated. Graduates from eastern Europe become porters in London; India and China produce millions of English-speaking graduates every year able to work anywhere. Global media and social media present the lifestyles and opportunities in the West around the world, making these faraway places less strange and scary. Financial deregulation means overseas workers can remit pay back home, and these flows now play a large role in transfers from developed countries to developing countries. There are also significant push factors in the form of destabilization of large parts of the world. The international drugs war has created social dislocation due to cartel-related lawlessness and violence. Regime change polices in the Middle East have been prosecuted with real wars in Libya, Syria, Iraq, Yemen, and Afghanistan and lethal drone strikes beyond the war zones. There are strict trade sanctions on a further list of countries in three continents. These polices have forced people to flee economic collapse and a real threat of injury and death.

Technology

Underlying the aforementioned trends are technological advances. They have supported and enabled business consolidation and globalization.

From the early 1970s, containerization dramatically reduced the costs of moving freight between rail, ship, and road. This made international trade cheaper and more efficient.

Improved transport made global travel easier. Low-cost air-travel has led to rapid growth, enabling greater movement of people and goods across the globe.

But, the biggest impact has been the dramatic development of telecoms and information technology (IT). It is now easy to communicate and share information around the world. To exploit the technology advances, there are business schools turning out MBA consultants to provide approaches and techniques including business process reengineering; outsourcing; Six Sigma; just in time; lean manufacturing; and total quality management.

This communication technology and other globalization enablers have freed corporations to reconfigure operations to the lowest-cost workforce or to jurisdictions with the weakest regulation or lowest taxes. It has also made it possible for corporations to grow much bigger and maintain control over its sprawling assets with ever fewer management staff.

Some Consequences

Industry concentration is a measure of the market share of the top few companies. A 2016 paper[2] concluded more than 75 percent of U.S. industries have experienced an increase in the concentration levels over the last two decades. Firms in industries with the largest increases in product market concentration have enjoyed higher profit margins, positive abnormal stock returns, and more profitable mergers and acquisition deals, suggesting that market power is an important source of profit. Let us take Canada as an example[3] for trends everywhere. In 1950, an average firm within the top 60 was five times as large as an average of all firms listed on the Toronto Stock Exchange. By 1990, that ratio had risen only a little from five to six. By 2012, the ratio was 23. This pattern is reflected at the global level. In most mature industries, half a dozen or less companies dominate and control the market worldwide.[4] In mining, Glencore Xstrata has a revenue of 200 billion U.S. dollars, then comes ArcelorMittal at 70 billion U.S. dollars, and by Rio Tinto and BHP Billiton they are down to 40 billion U.S. dollars. There are just two domestic consumer goods suppliers, P&G and Lever. Looking at the U.S. market: baby food, three companies, Abbott, Mead Johnson, and Nestlé, have 80 percent of the market; footwear, Nike has 30 percent share, the next less than six percent; tobacco, two companies with 83 percent share, and Reynolds just announced a merger with U.K. giant BAT; dishwashers, three companies with 65 percent share. Even relatively new industries are the same such as mobile phones with four companies dominating worldwide.

---

[2] Are US Industries Becoming More Concentrated? Gustavo Grullon, Yelena Larkin, and Roni Michaely October 2016.
[3] A Shrinking Universe: How Concentrated Corporate Power is Shaping Income Inequality in Canada. Jordan Brennan. November 2012.
[4] Euromonitor.

Flatter Organizational Structures

The *Wall Street Journal* ran an article on PepsiCo[5] Inc.'s Gemesa cookie business in Mexico. In the 1990s, the company ran with 12 employees per manager. In 2008, its factories operated with 56 employees per manager. They noted the changes have helped Gemesa improve its business results. That may be extreme, but another article analyzing S&P 500 company performance reported Sung Won Sohn, a former chief economist at Wells Fargo as saying "U.S. companies became leaner, meaner and hungrier." In 2007, S&P companies generated an average of 378,000 U.S. dollars in revenue for every employee. In 2016, that figure had risen 20 percent to 510,000 U.S. dollars.

Longer Working Weeks for Some

A 2015 London School of Economics (LSE) study into working hours[6] identified that in western European countries, the frequency of individuals working extreme hours has increased substantially, particularly among high-skilled male workers. The study points to the effects of globalization and to national labor regulations and welfare reforms. Of course, extreme working hours have health impacts, and in recognition of this, in 2019, the World Health Organization (WHO) added *burn-out* to the International Classification of Diseases.[7]

So How Is It Today?

These trends have impacted different industries at different rates and times. Manufacturing first, service industries later, and finally, public sector and charities. Universities are now less concerned with creating

---

[5] Overseeing More Employees With Fewer Managers. Consultants Are Urging Companies to Loosen Their Supervising Views, By George Anders. Updated March 24, 2008, 12:01 a.m. ET.

[6] Extreme Working Hours in Western Europe and North America: A New Aspect of Polarization. Anna S. Burger. LSE, May 2015.

[7] World Health Organization, May 2019 => https://who.int/mental_health/evidence/burn-out/en/

prepared minds and more with courses as profit centers, targeting market segments, making pricing decisions based on demand to maximize profit contribution.

The outcome is a concentration of business in fewer corporations and the concentration of work into fewer individuals. Corporations have consolidated into fewer giant multinational companies with a global presence in many different national economies. They have continually stripped out layers of management and non-core functions, and at the same time, provided some functions from global service centers rather than locally.

For the general population, wages and working hours have stagnated;[8] for professionals in corporations, there has been a growth of extreme working hours. Fewer professionals and managers with more responsibilities are working longer hours. Corporations have cut the workforce to the extent that everyone left is busy all the time, leaving no spare staff capacity.

So, how is it in today's corporate working environment compared to the 1980s? Change is constant. Organizational structures are flat and management teams are lean. Expectations for results are higher and time-frames are shorter. Senior managers spend less time in post, so they need to make their mark faster. Client contracts are shorter and pressure on prices greater. Decision-making time is shorter and projects need to happen faster. Service problems reach the media instantaneously, risking personal and business reputations.

Staff no longer smoke at their desk, they make their own tea, nine to five culture has been replaced by 24-hour availability, communication is instant and easy to send but often overwhelming to receive, the typing pool and admin staff are now a smartphone and a computer you take everywhere with you, and there are no Dans anymore. There are no managers between roles to run projects. It is a world of long commutes to 60-hour weeks, engaging in multiple careers in multiple companies without final salary pensions.

---

[8]   Pew Research https://pewresearch.org/fact-tank/2018/08/07/for-most-us-workers-real-wages-have-barely-budged-for-decades/

CHAPTER 4

The Changed Project Landscape

Project Management Thinking

People have been changing things using projects certainly since the rise of civilizations. Huge structures were built by the Greeks, Romans, and Egyptians thousands of years ago that are still with us today. Infrastructure on the scale of an airport or a high-speed rail link delivered without power tools. Possibly, it helped to have an endless supply of forced labor and an incentive scheme where a poor appraisal led to literal termination. However, this is not the old world we want to talk about. It does not relate to a specific period, as the change happened at different times in different industries and countries. The old world is how it was before the shareholder value revolution discussed in Chapter 3 and before the professionalization of project management as a discipline.

Before the drive for shareholder value increased the pace of business change, projects tended to take place away from the ongoing operations—organized as separate entities and resourced and managed accordingly. In most cases, there was also some form of project management office (PMO) to support the governance of multiple projects. In other areas, the organization tended to look after itself.

Projects were typically consecutive, rather than concurrent. Project managers arrived at a completion date based on the effort and duration required. There was acceptance that "things took that long."

The staffing of projects was also different in the old world. Particularly large or difficult projects involved the services of external consultancies as today, and as today, needed to involve lots of internal staff with domain knowledge. Smaller projects were staffed from the business. Before shareholder value pressures developed, there were personnel departments that considered staff as permanent features to be managed through a life-time career, so there were also plenty of people making their way on the management track being moved around from line jobs to overseas posts and back again to head office. For these rising managers, part of their career progression were periods as a "Special Projects Manager." These managers had experience of the business, its people, processes, and sys-tems and would also have the time to focus on the project.

This is how one of the authors came to this career. He ran a couple of projects and realized he was a project manager (PM). It turned out that he had the right attributes and so developed the technical skills and became full-time dedicated to the developing profession.

If you look back at our prologue project, many of the features of that project would have been different in the old landscape. For example, the PM might have been full time and dedicated and the project team mem-bers may have been seconded on to the project and taken out of their normal jobs.

But, the post shareholder value project landscape is not like this. Look again at the producer matrix in Chapter 3. In addition to increasing the efficiency, the business must address effectiveness—doing the things that add value to customers. Both these things require improvements to exist-ing operations. Such improvements require projects, but these projects now must be done in flattened-down and thinned-out organizations with human resource functions expert in ensuring the organization is always "rightsized." These projects now must be done in organizations without special PMs and with departments lean to the bone with staff already working extreme hours and no spare capacity. Such departments are often unwilling to second staff for months or even give them up for a few hours a day.

The context within which projects are run now is described earlier. There is an increasing pressure to deliver programs and projects much more quickly. In some cases, dates for delivery are set before projects are properly defined, and this causes more pressure on the balance of time, costs, and scope.

This pace of business change now means, often, several projects are taking place at the same time. Organizations have to multi-task, adding to the complexity and increasing the management challenge, forcing it to juggle demands on money and resources and time.

The Evolution of Project Management

In the old world, project management was not a concept familiar outside engineering and IT, and even in those spheres, there was a large variation in approaches to delivering projects. The UK Government was a good example of undertaking numerous engineering and IT projects which frequently overran, were over budget and didn't deliver to the customer's expectations. In 1983, to overcome this weakness in its project capability, it adopted a methodology called PROMPT II (Project Resource Organization Management Planning Techniques). In 1987, based on its experience with PROMPT II in practice, the methodology was enhanced and became PRINCE2. In 1990, keen to see improved project performance across government contracts and wider industry, the government placed the enhanced method into the public domain as an open method.

Table 4.1 shows how much change there has been in the evolution of the project management environment.

Methodologies and skills have responded to organizational pressures. The early 2000s saw the birth of the agile principles for software development. The science of project management is well served by these improvements, and that organizations are in a much better place to deliver projects of all types. However, our experience is that although composite projects are underpinned by these methodologies, there are specific issues that are overlooked. This book provides our insights into that missing knowledge and some of the art of project management for composite projects.

Table 4.1 The evolution of project management

Old world	New world
Techniques originated in IT and construction	Methodologies have evolved, PRINCE2 now in its fourth generation, kept up to date with modern day needs, birth of *agile*
Few accredited PMs	PM as a profession, accreditations under PRINCE2, APM, PPI
Few business change PMs	Readily available business change PMs
Dedicated project resources	Blend of dedicated resource and those with Business as Usual (BaU) responsibilities
Project work away from BaU	Work is in or close to the business or operation
PMO capability rare, except in the Level 1 projects	Enterprise PMO capability more common providing prioritization, budget control, and so on
You had more time; you could plan to a date	You are often given a date
Gantt charts consecutive	More work is concurrent, multiple business change projects
People waiting between jobs available for projects	No longer *spare* people
Genuine development	Business lead, change managers, subject matter experts with BaU responsibilities in addition
"Special Projects Manager" (SPM)	No longer *spare* people to tackle projects
SPM will have business knowledge	Specialist PMs may not have business knowledge
SPM unlikely to have PM skills	PM likely to be qualified, business support may not
In IT, it was a development from the business analyst role	PMs drawn from wider backgrounds
Failure was usually a secret	Failure more easily communicated

PART II

Implications

CHAPTER 5

Impact and the People Project Triangle

We have seen that the pace of business change has risen; this means the pace with which businesses need to respond with new and reconfigured assets and processes has risen. This is done with projects, so the need for more projects to deliver ever more quickly, effectively, and efficiently.

Fortunately, in response to this need, the project management discipline has professionalized. We now have well-researched and tried methods, tools, and techniques that increase the chance of project success.

Undermining this progress though is the continual competition for resources between projects and business as usual (BaU). This is true for all projects, but it is especially true for composite projects—those staffed with in-house people working on them part time. The result is ever-increasing pressure on those in-house staff.

Why is this important when everyone works under pressure and has too much to do? The key issue is composite project structures are a valuable way to run projects, but they should not happen by accident. Organizations using composite projects and unaware of the implications of these structures are exposed to unrecognized risks and unexpected problems. Organizations should be explicitly aware they are organizing a composite project structure and understand the implications of the decision. Then, they will be prepared to overcome some of the practical and organizational hurdles.

The seeds of problems are likely in place even before the appointment of a project manager, when the first-time project sponsor and business lead initiate the project as a supplement to their primary role. Right from the start, they are working outside their normal schedule. They are likely to be working at capacity and have to do extra hours, so will regard it as *homework*. It is then they create a composite project without realizing it, and without understanding the implications and the risks they are taking on. Risks that can be serious, for the organization and for the reputations of participants.

So, what are the implications? Project managers often use the project triangle concept to understand trade-offs and limitations of resourcing decisions between quality, time, cost, and scope. In composite projects, there is a higher level of trade-off between the people working on the project, the ongoing operations of the business, and the project itself. The next sections build on this concept to establish a clear understanding of why composite projects are different and what the implications are.

The Project Triangle

The *project triangle* or *iron triangle*, see Figure 5.1, is a tool that has been used by project managers for a long time, if not well known outside the discipline. It is used to describe the balance and trade-offs between constraints and risks.

The triangle shows the relationship between scope, time, and cost. The fourth variable, quality, anchors the others together. The key concept

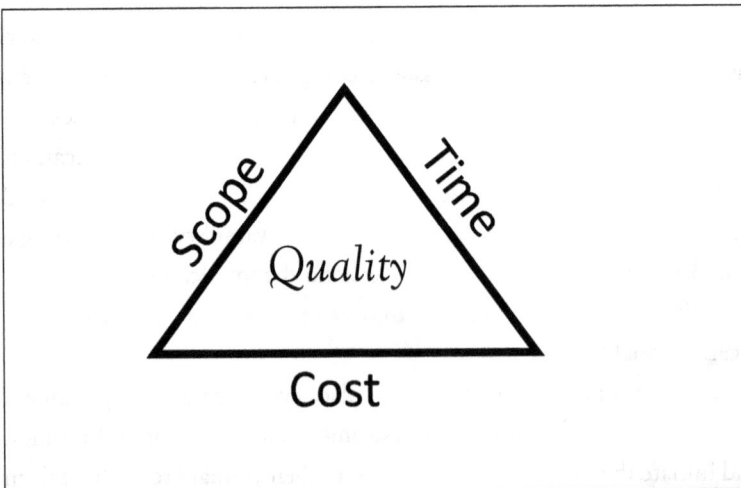

Figure 5.1 The project triangle

is that you cannot improve all the variables at once. Like a law of physics, at least one variable must give. For example, to deliver a project in less time, you must either reduce the scope, increase the cost, or both.

When managing a project, it is important to understand on which of the variables your project is focused and which can be compromised. Sometimes, it is obvious; many times, it is not. For example, if you are Boeing and the U.S. Federal Aviation Administration (FAA) has grounded one of your aircraft models until a safety upgrade is completed, the project is going to be focused on scope (fit the upgrade on all aircraft) and time (get it done as soon as possible). Cost will be the variable that is flexible because of the huge damage being done to the company while the aircraft are grounded.

For new software products, often, the launch date is important. This might be due to external factors like a product to meet the arrival of a new regulation or a game to hit the Christmas peak. It might be due to internal factors like meeting the expectations created by pre-launch publicity and marketing. In this case, time is the focus. However, cost may also be constrained, as there are diminishing returns on adding resources. So, the scope is likely to be the flexible variable with non-essential features pushed back into later releases.

As it is usually the last to be compromised, quality sits in the middle. You might reduce the number of deliverables (scope) in a project, but those left must work properly. Using a fanciful example, the intention might be to make a prestige five door car. If you run out of cash, you can still build a prestige three door car. However, there are times quality might be traded. For a building development, lower-cost heat insulation materials might be traded for higher utility bills during operation. Lower-quality fittings might be traded for shorter life and hence, higher lifetime costs.

This is a valuable framework, but business is about getting more from less. Determined and ambitious managers will always demand more features, more speed, and less cash. There is another law of nature that should be explicitly considered. There is a relationship between more risk and more reward.

As a hypothetical example, an organization wants to restructure its customer service operation that includes a management team and a call center. The project has been set up as follows:

- Scope is facilities and new job descriptions for 50 people, all posts subject to change, one location.
- Time is 3 months from announcement to new structure. Budget includes redeployment costs and a small amount of specialist external resource.
- The project is sponsored by the chief executive, but will be delivered by the human resources (HR) team, with support from operational managers.

On the face of it, the project is well planned. However, the chief executive becomes uncomfortable on the lead up to the announcement and, for sound reasons, feels that the time to launch is too long and will be very unsettling for the customer service team, and pose a risk to the operation. The project is now to be completed in two months.

So, considering the project triangle, what are the options?

- Reduce the scope by decreasing the number of people affected. This will reduce the amount of communication required and the face-to-face sessions with staff.
- Increase the cost by increasing the resources from HR available to the project. This might be by using overtime or buying in additional resources to support the HR team.

There is a third option:

- Reduce the time, make no changes to scope and cost, but increase risk.

The risks that you would identify for this project would be:

- Industrial relations issues reducing operational performance.
- Legal action resulting in legal costs.
- Overworked HR team, resulting in sickness or staff turnover.
- Operations managers lose focus, resulting in lower operational performance.

In practice, the option to reduce scope is unlikely to be feasible because a partial restructure is unlikely to deliver the business case. This leaves the option to increase spend or accept the risks shown earlier. It is a legitimate practice for a business to accept risks—it is an option in the PRINCE2 manual: providing it is done consciously and explicitly. Too frequently, blindly taking on risks like these typically just delays the inevitable. Antagonizing the team and overworking the HR department often incurs higher costs eventually, and maybe even higher costs than before.

Faced with challenges to scope, time, and cost, it is possible to use the project triangle along with an analysis of risk, as a tool to explicitly guide thinking.

Trade-offs and risk around composite projects are key themes of this book. In the rest of this chapter, we will add to your understanding of the composite project environment by building on this concept of the project triangle.

The Composite Project Environment

For project managers not used to composite project environments, the experience can be very frustrating. Much of this is organization culture mismatch. The demands and culture of a project-orientated department, such as IT, differ radically from the nature of operations or BaU. We introduced this in Part I, and the key differences are repeated in Table 5.1:

Table 5.1 Projects and BaU compared

Feature	BaU management	Project management
Responsibility	For status quo	For change
Authority	Defined by organizational structure	Fuzzy
Tasks	Consistent	Ever-changing
Stability	Permanent	Temporary
Focus	Efficiency	Conflict resolution and tradeoffs

Construction and IT projects tend to be more directly sequence-restricted; things must be done in a specific sequence. The concrete must set before the roof trusses can be put up. It does not matter how many people you throw at the task, the fact that concrete must set will not change. In the BaU world of service operations, for example, there is usually more flexibility over the order tasks that can be carried out, and often the option of *all hands on-deck* to solve a problem.

It is not surprising that when project-orientated people are mixed with BaU-orientated people, there is often misunderstanding and conflict. The two groups do not understand each other. As a project manager in a composite environment, it is essential you understand your BaU colleagues if you are to get the most out of them.

There are two broad categories of difference: cultural and practical.

Cultural

Organizations thrive because of the benefits of specialization of function. Staff in different disciplines have different skills and aptitudes and, of course, attitudes. Project specialists work in a way that is different to operations, marketing, or finance. In particular, departments with a never-ending, consistent output are orientated to stability over change; consistent repeat actions over unique tasks; and efficiency over innovation and trade-offs. An important cultural difference is that in BaU, being a *safe pair of hands* and not making mistakes is highly valued. This works against the need for innovation and flexibility that is needed and prized in projects.

For example, compared to project-oriented staff, operational staff:

- May be very impatient in meetings and want things to be done quickly, leading them to rush to solutions before the problem is fully assessed.
- May dismiss up-front thinking and planning as just delay and procrastination and so regard detail in project documents, like the requirements specification, as a waste of time.
- Think the project is going too slowly, that things could be done much quicker by avoiding the project bureaucracy.

- May have been volunteered for the role in the project because they have the specialist subject knowledge, but have no interest in delivery.
- May not understand project methodology and approaches and find it difficult to relate to them.

Practical

A project manager must realize that part-time operations staff on a project have a full-time job, against which they have performance targets and goals. Targets and goals they will be measured against come their annual review. Their time is limited, and their future is linked to their line manager not the project manager. This means operational issues will be prioritized over the part-time temporary project.

- If a customer or other operational emergency emerges, then staff probably will not appear at the requirements workshops or project meetings.
- There will be financial or operational or seasonal peak periods during the week, month, or year, which may mean you have to build the plan around them. Failure to do so will mean the BaU staff will not be available to the project.
- It is likely that the staff will have little time assigned to the project and so forced to schedule project work into an already busy week. It is common for them to think of their normal work responsibilities as the *day job*, and project work, perceived as outside normal responsibilities that they must do in addition, as *homework*. They might refer to their regular job as *real work*.
- Line managers may resent the time their staff are spending on the project.

Project management from traditional project environments such engineering and IT:

- May unreasonably expect project staff to understand project methodology and tools.
- Fail to tailor the project methodology to suit the composite structure and insist on strictly following the processes with unnecessary meetings and reports.
- Issue work packages that are too big or complex for the part-time staff to manage.
- Be frustrated by lack of direct line control over part-time staff and hence, attendance or late deliverables.
- Have experience dominated by repeater-type projects, which are projects like the last job, but with specific differences. For example, a building contractor has managed many housing developments in the past. All the main elements are well known and been done before, but the specifics must be managed, such as particular ground requirements, or particular suppliers. Business projects tend to be highly bespoke projects that are unique for the organization, such as create a new service, a relocation, a reorganization, or process change. These tend to have more uncertainty, but rigid deadlines.

Time and Mental Capacity

Another key issue for the composite project that we have emphasized already is simply the lack of time your BaU part-time staff have. One of the authors vividly remembers the first time he heard project work referred to as homework. He was working on a particularly contentious project in a large company, which required the consolidation and relocation of several contact centers. It was a stressful time for the experienced managers who ran these operations. In a meeting to discuss the approach, one of the senior managers complained that they were doing this project as homework, by which he meant he was having to do the work outside his normal workday, which was already fully scheduled. That phrase and its connotation has stayed with him ever since as he regularly works on projects where key people have a full-time day job too.

It is not just the time. People can hold only so much in their heads at a time. So many outstanding tasks, so many problems, too many worries. Switching between activities takes mental effort, especially if it is a different domain or different way of working. BaU part-time staff just might not have the time or mental capacity to devote to the project.

The People Project Triangle

Earlier, we described the standard project management tool of the project triangle and its use to understand the constraints and trade-offs in projects between the variables of scope, cost, and money. We then described the composite project environment where staff with full-time day jobs must accommodate additional project work. This places pressure on the people, which impacts the progress of the project and the ongoing business-as-usual activities. There becomes a trade-off among these constraints, and so, another triangle suggests itself, the people project triangle.

The people project triangle is presented in Figure 5.2. It shows the relationship between people, the business, and the project. Again, the key concept is that you cannot improve all the variables at once. When the pressure is on, you must decide which variables take priority and which are sacrificed.

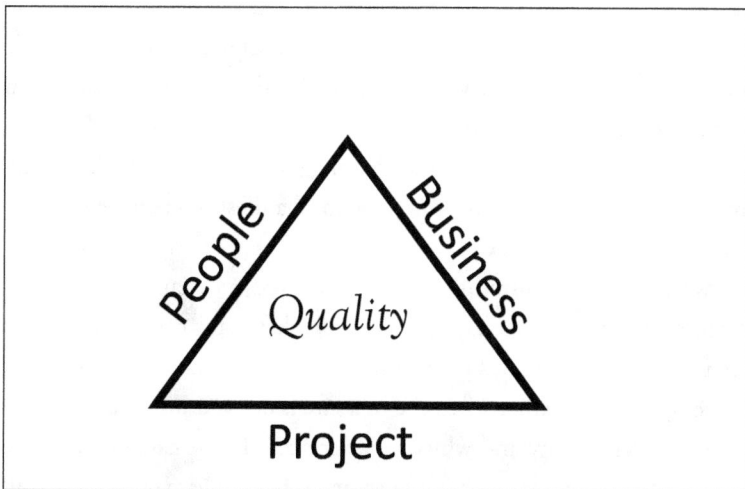

Figure 5.2 The people project triangle

As in the standard triangle, quality anchors the others together and sits in the middle. Quality here relates to *business* performance key performance indicators (KPIs); *project delivery* within budget, cost, and time; and *people's* quality of life.

The business as usual of transforming resources into outputs that customers value and demand must continue. Schedules have to be operated, performance has to be maintained, and customer expectations have to be met. This is the lifeblood of the organization. If existing commitments are not met, then there are short-term financial consequences and long-term reputation consequences. If sales targets are missed, there are medium-term financial consequences, and if marketing campaigns are delayed, there are long-term financial consequences. These are unyielding pressures. The staff, even if on a project as well, have to do their day job. If they do not, there is visible pain.

Composite projects come in all sizes with all levels of urgency and importance. They are not the most mission-critical projects, but delay or failure is likely to have severe consequences, not least for the managers involved. The organization and the individuals may suffer reputation damage and visible pain.

We have left the people who work in the organization and are seconded to work part time on projects until last, because they are often the least considered on the trio of variables. As discussed in Part I, the lean organization has left its staff with little slack, and yet, they are expected to add project workload into their schedule. As a consequence, there may be impacts. Staff who find they are struggling to deliver fear for their reputation and may turn inward and experience stress and anxiety. They may turn outward to voice malcontent affecting morale and staff turnover. The impact of stress and staff turnover may not manifest immediately, but can rumble on for a long time.

We recommend introducing the people project triangle, to bring to the foreground and make explicit trade-offs that many organizations have been making unconsciously and implicitly rather than consciously and explicitly. We said earlier when the pressure is on, you must decide which variables take priority and which are sacrificed. In the case of composite projects, our experience is that management is not aware of this trade-off, and the consequence is that it is nearly always the people who take the strain and suffer the consequences.

In the rest of Part II, we will explore in detail the impact and risks associated in these three dimensions: the people who work in the organization, the business as usual, and the composite project.

CHAPTER 6

Impact on People

Individual Reputation

Individual reputation is how an individual is perceived in the organization and, therefore, impacts relationships and power with their subordinates, peers, and managers. For senior managers, this includes their relationship with the board.

This book is making the case that unrecognized composite projects present risks greater than their strategic value might suggest. Level 3 tactical projects are not big enough to affect the organization or make the news externally. Level 1 strategic projects are recognized as being big enough to impact the business and so, typically, have strong governance. This makes them less likely to fail, and when they do, the symptoms are noticed and eventual failure anticipated, even if sometimes the outcome is still spectacular. Unrecognized composite projects may not have the governance and so, may fail spectacularly and unexpectedly. Cost, time, and scope do not often make the news, but a quality failure might. This means that for the managers involved, unrecognized composite projects represent increased risk to personal reputation. We are particularly concerned with managers acting as sponsors, work-stream leaders, and subject-matter experts.

We discussed earlier the difference in cultures between projectized departments and business-as-usual (BaU) departments and what things are valued in each environment. We see this is reflected in the personal characteristics that are valued in managers and how individual reputations are built.

Project managers are valued for their ability to respond to an ever-changing situation and be highly tolerant to uncertainty—they are doing something that has not been done before. Things can be bruising for project managers when tasks do not come in on time or do not work as expected. Project managers must be task-focused, and to solve problems, need to be politically aware and cool under pressure. They must excel at communication and motivating others who they can only influence and not command.

For people drawn from the business, the BaU job is about consistency and efficiency. The focus is on avoiding mistakes rather than innovation. Personal reputation centers around being a *safe pair of hands*, someone who can *get things done*, and the *go to* person for a subject. Careers progress by having ever more people and resources to run efficiently and by ever more autonomy over those resources. This is granted only when things do not go wrong. A normal life in a project replete with issues, risks, delays, and calls for extra cash is not familiar and comfortable with people used to BaU challenges. Particularly, at the board level, people are expected to hit targets and so, asking for more time or money is excruciating for sponsors and business leads. This is not an experience they will expose themselves to lightly. They are likely to want involvement in projects to the extent they enhance prospects for their main career in the BaU environment. This means enhancing not undermining their reputations.

You might think being part of a successful project can only enhance reputations. It is likely, but composite project involvement may just be overlooked and *go under the radar*. It is particularly likely the sheer amount of effort required will not be appreciated.

Disappointing or failed projects certainly do not grow reputations, especially for those highly involved with the project such as project sponsors and business leads.

So, how robust are the reputations of such BaU managers? What is their risk? This depends on where they stand at the time.

Strong reputations generally survive a problematic composite project because it is only part of the manager's remit, which is otherwise performing, or if the project is perceived to be difficult. However, for someone building a reputation, this will not be the case and they might suffer a serious impact.

So, from the perspective of BaU managers, they might perceive composite project involvement has asymmetrical risk. They suffer reputation damage if it fails, their career *takes a hit*, but may achieve little upside if it succeeds.

Project managers need to be aware of this dynamic when trying to influence such managers. But also, organizations need to be aware of this dynamic when setting up composite projects and drafting reluctant BaU managers. It may have invisible costs in terms of performance of the project and well-being of the managers.

Story: Reputation, Reputation, Reputation

The following story is not really a story—it is an illustrative scenario showing the impact of a badly performing project on individual reputations.

Project Kark Rash in the Prologue is fictional example of a project that underperformed and affected both BaU and the team's well-being. The project team members are unlikely to volunteer for another project, but their reputations would probably remain intact. However, the reputations of the project sponsor, the business lead, and the project manager would probably not.

It is not that they would be fired—it is more subtle than that. After all, these are good managers, and they would have made sure their BaU objectives were achieved. The meetings with senior stakeholders would have been very uncomfortable as they reported issues and requested additional budget, or time, or a reduction in scope. Sometimes, stakeholders perceive these requests as failure, and so. there would have been an air of disappointment around the room.

To their peers, they are associated with a project that has become a laughingstock, even if their day job is performing fantastically well. Yes, they would have had a bit of a laugh and joke about it, but the perception sticks.

It is a fact of life that many projects run into problems; we have been in these meetings and observed these conversations. We also see how tricky it is for those individuals at the time and understand their concern about the effect on their next opportunity for promotion.

Impact on the Individual

We have discussed that for people drawn from BaU, their job focused on consistency and efficiency does not prepare them for a composite project environment full of setbacks and change.

What are some other features of the composite project environment that pose difficulties for the BaU staff?

- Operational staff are used to resolving problems quickly, then moving on to the next one. They are busy, and their time is not their own; it is dictated by events in many cases. They may be frustrated by the slow pace of the project environment.
- They inevitably experience conflict over time choices between BaU and the project. They may feel stress from the pressure of being chased for both and paid (appraised) for only one.
- BaU staff may bring with them emotional scars from earlier outside initiatives that did not deliver or brought them grief.
- Project timescales are often different to operational timescales.
- Projects need to be set up properly, and that can take some time. Operational staff cannot understand why "we can't just get on with it."
- They work with people who are not their direct reports. They are used to the levers that come with direct organizational authority. Responsibility without direct authority can be stressful if that is not what you are used to.
- Some of the frustrations of project life include changing timescales, inter-department working where they do not have the line management to back them up, and finding themselves involved in a struggling project. An issue for many is that sometimes, their unexpected project homework falls outside of their plan for the week.
- One of the most stressful things for all people is a sense of not being in control of one's life. BaU managers may feel this when they have been effectively conscripted onto the project, possibly because the senior management has decided they

are the most knowledgeable and experienced person in the subject matter. Stress is amplified if they are not fully behind the project or fear it may fail.

- The project methodology can be an issue too. It is common for people running operations to understand the need for good governance, but still be frustrated by it. In rare cases, it could be the other way around. Certainly, the unnecessarily rigid adherence to detailed project methodology is not good for the project. For example, how does a project manager schedule a resource that is already 100 percent committed?

- All these stress factors are magnified by lengthy involvement. More than 3 to 9 months on a project can start to feel like a life sentence.

Projects can, of course, have a positive impact on individuals. Association with successful outcomes can boost careers. Morale and motivation can be enhanced by the challenge and exposure to something different and new. Also, projects help managers adapt to the new and as the cliché *change is a constant* is probably true; this is an important skill. Notwithstanding the *glow* from being part of successful projects, perversely, people will learn more from a difficult and problematic project than from an easy one. They just might not appreciate it at the time.

But, the risk for organizations is that projects have a negative impact on individuals. The negative impacts are mostly related to managers already working at capacity, being handed additional project work to *fit in* with their schedule. This effect is increased when the project starts to have difficulties forcing unplanned extended periods of long working hours.

It is reasonable to assume people come to work to do a good job and are usually diligent and will carry out their work on both BaU and the project, but time pressures can lead to skimping or neglecting BaU responsibilities. This can often be an issue if project deadlines clash with the BaU diary, for example, at the month end. This can mean reputation impact for their core role, as discussed earlier. Performance assessment goals are likely to be around this and not the project, especially if the line manager is not benefiting from the project. These conflicting priorities between bosses is particularly stressful.

The time commitment and mental capacity issues do not just relate to the project tasks the BaU manager is assigned. Any project requires them to learn the project way of working—meetings, work packages, reporting, and so on. The governance process may be unfamiliar and frustrating. They may have to learn the terminology and concepts of this new discipline: critical path, dependencies, risk management, and the rest.

A composite project is even more complex, as it involves managing time and priorities between BaU and the project. It also may involve working with other team members juggling time, but with a different monthly BaU cycle. For example, we have seen a company month end that requires some teams to work flat out on the run up to month end, while other teams run flat out the week after.

A failing composite project exaggerates all the demands and adds others. There will be extra work for the project, potential unpaid overtime with loss of time from the BaU day job. They have to re-plan their BaU diary, do more delegation, use more backfill resource, and limit the support they can give to their BaU team. It is rarely feasible for the regular BaU tasks to be canceled or even delayed, and line managers sometimes refuse extra time on project work and limit the time spent to the time originally agreed. The staff member can feel a risk to their sense of professionalism with respect to achieving deadlines or producing quality work.

Under pressure, managers may project outward, impacting morale and motivation, which can infect the staff around them. Alternatively, managers may project internally, which manifests as stress and anxiety with corresponding consequences for physical and mental health. These consequences may not manifest immediately, making it hard to connect to the cause. Mental health issues can fester for a very long time before erupting in sickness days or resignation.

Negative impact on individuals is likely to manifest as negative impact on the business at some time. The most visible is sickness days or staff turnover. But, there is less visible pain. Managers may never want to do another project again, or they start resentful or unmotivated next time round.

Story: Contact Center Concern

The following story illustrates many of the features of the composite project environment that poses difficulties for the BaU staff. In this example, several of the project team members had to contend with *life on a project,* while at the same time, their job roles were changing. A large UK organization embarked on a project to consolidate multiple call centers into a new operation. One of the authors took on the role of project manager, starting from the point a supplier was named *preferred bidder,* until the new consolidated operation was live.

The organization decided to pull together call centers from its business units, under a new supplier. This was a significant shift in strategy and came with challenges because the business units did not all support the consolidation. They marketed themselves as unique businesses and were suspicious of changes to combine *back office* functions.

In addition, the current managers were fairly *hands on* with the operations, even though the staff worked for their suppliers. The new strategy meant that these managers would become *supplier* managers, rather than *operational* managers. For example, instead of managing a large local call center, they would be remotely managing the new supplier.

As is sometimes the case in a difficult business change, the key stakeholders and project team members were not all supportive of the change, or the effect on their roles. On top of that, they were a vital part of this lengthy, composite project because of their unique operational knowledge and experience. At a time when people in their own teams were most unsettled, they were having to spend time on critical project tasks. It is easy to understand the pressures and internal conflicts.

The tensions of this situation led to some people being quite difficult to work with on the project. They challenged the principles behind the plan at every stage. They were highly critical of the inbound supplier, right from their appointment and throughout the implementation. In meetings, while remaining professional, they were very disruptive. The project leadership team were kept busy trying to keep on track and avoid a mutiny.

In this case, despite the difficulties, the consolidated call center opened on time and the necessary changes were made to the old organizational structure. But, most people involved were left rather bruised from the experience.

On refection, the key learning from this project was that it is vital to try to really understand the impact of the change on all those whose support you need. You must think hard about how they might be feeling and how they might react as part of the project team.

CHAPTER 7

Impact on Business as Usual

Organizational Performance

In our experience with composite projects, staff are seconded by business-as-usual (BaU) line managers to project work on the understanding that their primary role is not neglected. Their attitude is liable to be that they are lending the staff member's time, almost as a favor. But we have already identified that in the modern corporation, staff are already at near capacity, so often, there is eventual conflict over time allocation. In that fight BaU, usually wins for several reasons. There is a cultural aspect: the individuals and their managers have an expectation that their primary role is critical and must not falter. This is supported by structural elements, such as business and personal objectives not including the project outputs. The attitude is revealed in conservations when people refer to their *real work*, that is, their normal work commitments outside the project. The phrase, itself, reveals what they consider to be important, and hence, given priority.

However, it is not always the project that misses out and so, there are risks. We have largely focused on staff capacity in terms of time, but there is also the effect of mental capacity, or as it is sometimes referred to *head space*. Regardless of time, there is simply only a limited amount of issues a person can think about at a time. It is hard to pin a specific business impact to a specific project cause, and sometimes, the day job is achieved in the short term, but issues occur in the medium term.

BaU Risk of Not Receiving Process Improvements

Business operations must continually improve to stand still in the market. It is successful projects that deliver these improvements. So, failure to run successful composite projects threatens BaU in the long term.

Line managers who do not enable their staff the time and space to contribute may see it as a *win*, but this is only in the short term. In the long term, if they compromise projects delivering BaU improvements, then eventually, they lose.

Risk of BaU Under-Performance Through Lost Resources During the Project

If BaU is under-resourced during composite projects, there is the risk of late reports, missed regular meetings, increased customer complaints, reduced speed of response, and deterioration of other operational key performance indicators (KPIs). Obvious impacts of poor business performance are increased costs, reduced revenue, or customer satisfaction and corresponding impact on organizational reputations.

The occasions this most often happens, when BaU resources become focused on the project, are when the composite project runs into difficulties. It is then the project absorbs more time and reduces focus on BaU.

Impact on the Staff Performance

Chapter 6 discussed the impact on staff. Many of the negative impacts on staff feed through to negative impacts on the organization.

- Key people may not wish to be involved in projects again, which hurts the business long term.
- Staff turnover—that invisible pain may only manifest itself when key people decide to leave.
- Staff dissatisfaction and morale, which can spread and impact general performance and turnover.

Story: Payment System Pain

The following story illustrates the pain created in the organization from a project that runs into difficulties. In this case, the key project team members were managers from the payment departments.

A large UK company embarked on a program of projects to improve the efficiency and security of the process it used to transfer monies to its outlets. The program ran for multiple years and delivered several significant process and system improvements. One of those, a new module, proved to be extremely troublesome. It was designed to automate part of the process and improve financial control.

One of the authors ran the program from its inception. This project was the last for the overall program. On the face of it, things were going along well. The team had created a detailed set of requirements, the supplier was selected via a sound purchasing process, had done good work in the past, their design looked good, and so on.

We reached the user acceptance test (UAT) phase on the plan. A UAT confirms the business need has been met by the software. We required two weeks' work from each of the department managers. The deep knowledge was embedded in these people and so, we had no choice about who could test. We had to be as efficient as possible with their time, so the UAT was planned with precision—scheduled to avoid month end, holidays, and so on.

However, the software was not of a quality suitable for UAT. The reasons were part of the detailed post-project review and are not relevant here. It meant that several further rounds of user testing were required. The payment managers understood the need for more testing and the need for their involvement but were exasperated. Not only was this more time away from BaU, but the new module would be late too. Their managers were even less impressed.

Arranging the extra testing was straightforward on a practical level. However, we had lost a great deal of support from the business. It was hard to convince them that the same thing would not happen again. They were reluctant to allow their staff to test again without guarantees about the software quality. The testers were also very disappointed and, understandably, became less motivated within the project and had to catch up on their day job.

Problems can occur in any project, but with a composite project, there may be additional risks to an organization's performance. In this case, the unplanned additional involvement of the payment managers posed a risk to the accurate and efficient running of their department

Organizational Reputation

As stated earlier, unrecognized composite projects present unrecognized risks. The size of Level 3 tactical projects means bad outcomes are contained. Level 1 strategic projects are big enough to have strong governance and so, bad outcomes are anticipated and managed. Unrecognized composite projects often lack strong governance, and so are prone to fail unexpectedly. The most frequent reputational damage comes from quality failure.

Organization reputation is synonymous with brand strength. It is won over many years from the many customer interactions and from media influence. Reputation is built when operational delivery matches or exceeds two key things: the promise made by marketing and public relations (PR) messaging and comparison with competition.

Importance of Organization Reputation

The organization's reputation or brand is a key asset.

- The stronger the brand, the lower price elasticity; in other words, the more it can charge for its products and services. A strong brand provides long-term revenue protection and potential growth.
- The goodwill built with customers shields them somewhat when errors are made. Customers tend to give the benefit of the doubt to a company with a strong reputation. This reduces switching and the cost of remedy.

How Robust Are Reputations?

Strong reputations can survive operational mistakes. In fact, from a foundation of trust with the customer, making a mistake and doing a good job of correcting it can enhance reputation: say sorry, explain, fix the problem, and compensate.

However, some types of failures quickly erode reputations. Data breaches are damaging because they point to a process failure and a lack of care over customer information. Failure of business change projects represent an own goal, a kind of planned failure. This shows poor management. Finally, a breach of core brand values can be highly disruptive. Take the example of Arthur Andersen, founded in 1913, and by 2001, one of the big five accounting firms in the world with revenues of nine billion U.S. dollars. For much of its history maintained an enviable reputation for high standards and honesty, with a commitment to the investors over its clients. However, in 2001, a major client, energy giant Enron, was found to have misreported 100 billion U.S. dollars in revenue through institutional and systematic accounting fraud resulting in its collapse and huge losses for investors and employees. Arthur Andersen was seen to have failed to have upheld standards of competency and honesty. Its reputation was shredded, its clients deserted it, and within months, it ceased to exist.

Projects and Their Impact on Reputations

Successful projects do not make the news, such as the switch of Eurostar from Waterloo to St Pancras Station in London and the London 2012 Olympic infrastructure. Failures often do; you will all have examples such as the introduction of New Coke, the Ford Edsel, BP Oil Spill in the Gulf of Mexico, or the opening of London Heathrow Terminal 5. These projects lost billions and had a major impact on the long-term reputation of the organizations involved. Of course, these problems arise from failure of risk assessments of Level 1 projects, but they do illustrate the threat to organizations that do not understand the risks they are taking on.

Story: Operational Resilience

The following story illustrates how precious an organization's reputation is and how people will go to great lengths to protect it.

A large organization had suffered two very costly reputational hits within a two year period. They were an integral part of the country's national infrastructure. Two years later, they were required to perform a key role as part of a global sporting event. To this end, and given the worldwide exposure, they embarked on a project to ensure their operation could deliver a truly excellent experience, for tens of thousands of extra visitors, for the duration of the event. For the senior team, they recognized they faced a potential *three strikes and you're out*. They also knew they were facing a hostile media and predicted high levels of scrutiny.

A year before the event, the organization put together a high-level plan. Delivery was to be a joint effort with their key long-term suppliers. One of the authors was engaged by one of them to help design their work package plan and implement it. There was a real buzz because of the nature of the event, and perversely, that people outside thought it could not be done.

Using the project triangle idea for this story, the quality of the planned operation was a given. The scope was non-negotiable and time was fixed. The senior team were going to protect or enhance the organization's reputation at all costs. Therefore, it is easy to see which dimension was the variable. Having said that, there was obviously a need to prove value for money for the planned solution.

The work ran for a year, and it was obvious throughout that reputation was the key driver against which all big decisions were judged. Budget requests were rigorously examined, but when push came to shove, reputation won. The combined effort of the teams involved proved the doubters wrong. The scale of the job was immense, and the compliance need was strict. But, the project implemented successfully and customer service levels over the period were the best they had ever measured.

CHAPTER 8

Impact on Projects

Projects structured as composite have higher risks than other forms of project. The risk comes from the inherent tension between the elements of the people project triangle: the demands on the project to schedule tasks using part-time staff resources; the need to keep BaU functioning with less staff capacity, both time and focus; and the pressure on the staff who are usually already at capacity and expected to fit in extra project work.

The pain is visible and experienced by everyone involved in the project and the business.

The Project Triangle

The project can experience unbudgeted costs because of increased task effort or duration, rushed work, and hence, rework.

Overrunning timescales because milestones are missed, some unrecoverable, which delays project delivery. People say, "I need to do some real work, back on the day job," because BaU needs to take precedence. On lengthy projects, senior managers can lose focus and do not let their people fully work on the project.

Scope reduction is a frequent response to cost and time over run. Features must be compromised to hit deadlines.

Quality, sometimes, is compromised to save costs, for example, use lower-quality furniture with shorter life on a refit.

Business Case Undermined

This is a common outcome for composite projects with inadequate governance. The business benefits are not delivered as expected or the benefits are delivered, but they do not provide a return because either it cost more, or it was late, or both. These may not be apparent during the project or ever. Sometimes, it is realized a while after the project was finished and maybe lost on the project team. This outcome is demoralizing for the team, and if common, slowly undermines the business.

Impact of Future Projects

Any of these outcomes has a long-term corrosive effect on the business. Confidence in projects becomes undermined, and they get a bad name. Then, people are reluctant to be involved again, or even the first time. They are concerned about stories from the past projects, about the time involved, and the damaged reputations of people who did.

Story: BaU Effect on the Business Lead

The following story illustrates how the demands of business as usual (BaU) may draw key people away from a composite project and how the risk of this should inform the selection of the project leadership.
A large UK organization, which was a specialist in providing operational services, renewed a contract with one of its major customers. For the renewal, they also took on additional scope that required the due diligence of the new business and the transfer in of a skilled team from the outgoing supplier. As always, the customer's expectation was, rightly, that the day-to-day operation was not to be affected by the start of the new contract.

One of the authors was engaged to manage the operational transition on behalf of the supplier (who was actually a regular client). The requirement was for strong stakeholder management skills and experience, with the normal technical skills a given. The original intention was that the supplier business lead would spend most of their time working on the transition. However, BaU came calling, and their time was reduced by about half. The business lead was integral to the process of onboarding the new team and in the final commercial contract. They were also the key point of contact for the customer and so, time on site was important.

As with most composite projects, the knowledge and experience of the business lead was such that they could not be replaced. In this case, the perceived risk to BaU was higher than the risk to the project. Risks to the project included poor customer management, reduced time spent with transferring staff, and a late contract.

However, right from the start of the project, it was recognized that the business lead may be dragged temporarily into other work. Therefore, care was taken in the selection of the project manager, and subsequent setup of the project reduced the risk. It was important that the onsite project team was able to properly represent the supplier in front of their customer.

In practical terms, this meant creating a realistic plan that effectively used the limited time available and careful diary management of supplier, customer, and inbound staff. It also meant agreeing a deal with BaU that we might want priority where there were unexpected and serious issues. This proved to be the case a couple of times, but the pragmatic approach resulted in delivery of a successful outcome.

CHAPTER 9

Thesis and Problem Summarized

Part I of this book charted changes in the business environment over the last few decades and the impact on the project environment.

Part II investigated the implications of these changes with reference to our concept of the people project triangle, on the success of projects, the consequences for the ongoing business, and in particular, the pressure on staff of the modern corporation.

From this, we learned the modern business environment is one of rapid change. The modern corporation is lean and very cost conscious. A consequence is an increasingly common project management situation of a medium important, medium complex business change project that cannot justify a full-time team. Instead, it is largely staffed by in-house resources working on the project in *addition* to their normal responsibilities. We term these composite projects.

The thesis of the book is that composite projects are being used at an increasing rate to meet the demands of rapid business change. However, they are largely unrecognized as a separate organizational category of project with particular characteristics, management needs, and risks.

Analogous to the classic project *Iron Triangle*, where there is a trade-off between cost, time, and scope, we maintain that there is a People Project Triangle. This is a trade-off between the project, the ongoing business, and the people working in both the business and the project.

When pressure mounts, generally, only two of those can be prioritized and one must give. We observe that it is often the people who bear the brunt with subsequence implications of stress and burnout.

However, with better recognition, clearer understanding, and appropriate measures, many of the common problems with composite projects can be foreseen and mitigated or avoided.

The remainder of the book, Part III, looks at what to do about it. A framework is provided for identifying when composite projects can be used. Then, a series of chapters recommending practical techniques and approaches for dealing with the implications identified in Part II are provided.

The basis of our recommendations is our own meandering experience, over decades in the field, across varied organizations and sectors. What we say may come across as highly prescriptive, and if this is the case, it is because these approaches have worked for us. However, we recognize this is an under-researched topic, and other managers may find approaches that work better for them and their organization. We hope this is the start of conversation, research, and experimentation into a neglected topic.

We have found several principles, techniques, and ways of working to mitigate the risk of composite projects, and Part III takes you through them covering:

- How to identify composite projects, and this alone will go a long way in deflecting many problems.
- The type of support you need before you start.
- How to make it easier for your project team.
- How to adapt the methodologies.
- Practical tips and advice.

PART III

What To Do

CHAPTER 10

Categorizing Projects

Categorizing Your Project

Before you can successfully manage a composite project, you must realize you have one; so, the first task is determining what category of project you have: Level 1, Level 2, or Level 3. These are not absolute categories, as they are relative to your organization and its experience with projects. Consider the project's complexity, criticality, and budget. You can use Figure 10.1 to guide you.

Complexity

Consider projects your organization has successfully completed or routinely undertakes. How complex is the project compared to those?

If the project is a core strategic initiative or involves major cross-company or inter-company supply chain business transformation, then it is sure to be Level 1. Also, relative to your usual projects, does it involve more departments, a wider range of cross-disciplinary skills, or more coordinated work streams? If yes, then you probably are dealing with a project that should be organized as Level 1.

If the impact of the project is contained within one department and the implementation skills required live within the department, then you have a Level 3 project.

Criticality

Next, consider the impact of success or failure of the project. How far across the organization will the impact be felt? If it is material to the

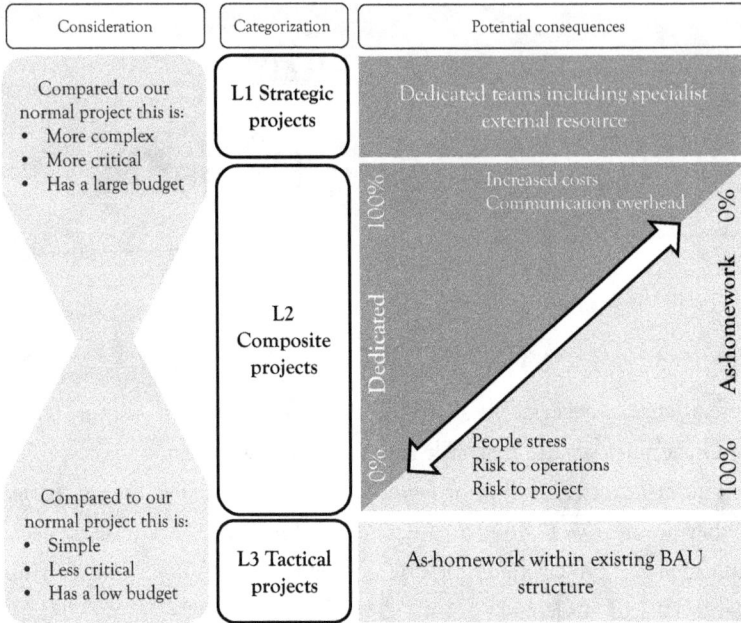

Figure 10.1 *Determining the dedicated or as-homework mix on your project*

annual profit, then the project is Level 1. If the gains or losses would only be noticed at department level, then the project is Level 3.

Budget

If the budget for the project is toward the top end of project budgets for your organization historically, then you are likely to need to organize as a Level 1. However, if the project falls within the department discretionary budget, it is probably Level 3.

Bringing It Together

If consideration of *any* of complexity, criticality, or budget is considered Level 1, then Level 1 organization is desirable. Only if *all* complexity, criticality, or budget considerations are Level 3 is the project likely to be easily organized as a Level 3.

After considering complexity, criticality, or budget and you do not have a Level 1 or a Level 3 project, then you have a Level 2 composite project. It will be a composite with a mix of dedicated and part-time staff with ongoing business-as-usual (BaU) commitments.

What Do We Mean by Dedicated?

Dedicated staff are people whose sole focus in the company is the project. They have no BaU responsibilities and no internal line managers. They could come from the company and be seconded on to the project or be external contractors.

As-homework staff are people who have BaU responsibilities in the company and line managers to report to for the BaU. Line managers who expect the BaU to continue as usual—products and services delivered to customers, end-of-quarter reports produced, performance reviews undertaken, and so on.

Full Time and Part Time

While an as-homework resource is, by definition, internal and part time, a dedicated resource can be either full time or part time. This is because an external resource can be part time, for example, two days a week, but when they are at the company, their only focus is the project. They have no internal line manager to answer to and no company BaU commitments.

How Is a Level 2 Composite Project Resourced?

For the purposes of this book, we use the following terminology to describe the project team. There is a *project sponsor* who provides the resources and is responsible for realizing the project benefits; a *business lead* responsible for the business changes once the other project deliverables are in place; and a *project manager* who manages the project. *Workstreams* are sub-projects, led by a *workstream lead* and supported by *workstream members* and subject matter experts (SMEs).

In the agile world, the project sponsor equates to the *product owner*; the project manager equates to the *scrum master*; the workstream lead and workstream members equate to the *team members*. The business lead is responsible for business changes, irrespective of the techniques used to create project outputs.

Sponsor and business leads: The nature of these project roles means they are always part time.

SMEs: These are usually as-homework and bought in to offer advice as needed.

Project manager and work stream leads: Can either be dedicated or as-homework resources. These are the first roles to be assigned as dedicated and the easiest to outsource to external project management professionals. Project management is a specialist skill the project will almost certainly benefit from someone with this training and experience. Additionally, the project needs a champion. Someone with a partisan interest in the success of the project, and only the success of the project, undiluted by considerations and internal politics from other organizations considerations.

Team members, the doers: a mix of dedicated and as-homework resources.

Pros and Cons for a High Dedicated Mix

A dedicated team focused on the single task of delivering the desired outcome is the most effective way to ensure it gets done. This is achieved by incurring the increased costs of those dedicated resources. The other key cost relates to communication overhead. Unless the dedicated team is all drawn from the business areas affected, then they will need to learn about the business and a lot of that learning will be from the staff in the business.

Pros and Cons for High As-Homework Mix

A dedicated team is expensive. An as-homework resource is expected to *fit in* the extra work around their normal work, but of course, there are not many staff in modern lean organizations with spare capacity to tap.

Alternatively, in many cases, the people with the skills, knowledge, and experience for the project cannot easily have their BaU roles covered by other in-house or external people.

So, as discussed elsewhere on the people project triangle, this form of organization comes with the risk of damage to either the staff resulting in stress, the operations or BaU because it is neglected, or if the staff cannot spend enough time on the project, then the project suffers from compromised quality, slipped timescales, or scaled back scope.

As you go into your project and design its organization structure, it is important to go in with your eyes wide open. Projects as-homework are a fact of modern business and will have to be done. We hope to make you aware of the risks so that you can look out for them and to give you some idea of the ways we have found to temper those risks as far as possible.

Story: Compliance Conundrum

The following story illustrates how important it is to recognize a composite project and, then, to ensure it is resourced appropriately.

A UK importer of consumer goods was wrestling with new government rules affecting the products in their sector. The manufacturer of those products had to increase the amount of testing done on its goods. It was having a big detrimental effect on its ability to meet demand in its markets across the world. One of the authors was engaged by the importer to help plan out the work required to overcome the supply issues.

There was an initial workshop to dig down into the detail of the issues faced. It was causing pain across all areas of the business. A second workshop was run with 20 senior managers with the objective of identifying solutions, resources, and approximate timescales.

The proposed project was complex and critical to the future of the organization. However, what was apparent very early on was that for the work required, we needed the expertise of a big group of people around the business. These key people were in separate small teams, so it was virtually impossible to backfill their roles while they were attached to the project. It was clearly a composite project, and so, we needed to find a way to support the business while this additional work was ongoing.

It is easy for people to claim they require more resources and easy for organizations to say no. In this case, the detailed work following the second workshop provided the evidence that the project would break BaU without changes to timetable, or additional resources or funding. The option to slip deadlines was not available because they were legislative.

In this case, the diagnosis as a composite project allowed the importer to set its priorities for the rest of the year. This enabled the business to adopt tactics to protect BaU performance, ensure that the project was delivered, and reduce the risk that people were completely frazzled.

CHAPTER 11

Executive Sponsor Is Key

The *sponsor*, in Project Management Institute (PMI) terminology, or the *executive*, in PRINCE2 terminology, is the person responsible for the project business case and ultimate delivery of the project benefits.

The sponsor has a strategic role in the project. They report upward to the company board on project progress and status and provide leadership to the project team. Their key functions are to provide resources, set the objectives and vision, appoint project board members and the project manager, and work with the team to overcome the large issues like budget and scope changes.

Story: Clear Roles

The following story illustrates the need for three key roles for a composite project, led by the project sponsor, and the importance of clear role descriptions.

A large UK organization embarked on a project to centralize one of its regional operations into a new building. The construction was halfway through, so the time had come to design and implement the internal fabric, devise the business processes, recruit the team, and so on.

The project sponsor and the business lead were in place. They had led the project during the initial construction phase where a supplier was engaged to project manage the build. The assumption was that the business lead would be able to handle project management for the design and implementation phase too. The work streams were agreed and the members informed, and an opening date was set (in stone).

The business lead had other responsibilities; so, even with the skills, there was little hope that the project management role was possible. This was an undiagnosed composite project.

However, quite early on in this phase, it was apparent that the combination of business-as-usual (BaU) and a project as-homework was not working, and the flag was raised. One of the authors was engaged to take on the role of the project manager. We completed a review of roles for the project leadership group straight away and our established rules of engagement.

The project sponsor and the business lead were freed up to spend more time supporting some nervous key stakeholders whose roles were changing as a result of the wider change. They took on the senior stakeholder management and purchasing duties for new suppliers joining the new operation.

It was not plain sailing to opening day, but with the support of the project leadership trio, the training operation was opened on time.

Even though they may have strong opinions on the subject, project managers rarely have any say in the choice of the sponsor for their projects. It is one of those factors, among many, that a project manager cannot control, but must do their best to manage. So, this section also addresses company boards selecting sponsors and the sponsors themselves.

The sponsor needs some key organizational and personal qualities if they are to be effective in championing the project. They need to support the project team with both practical and motivational activity. They may have to do this against a backdrop of indifferent or skeptical BaU managers that the team members work for when they are not on the project.

It is usually crucial they have hierarchal power with a title like chief, director, or head. However, beyond the title, a strong reputation or credibility goes a long way in smoothing the passage of a project, as it inevitably consumes jealously guarded resources and creates disruption to BaU processes and priorities. In other words, they must have the clout to unblock obstacles and free the project to move forward.

Sponsors are, of course, professionals who should be expected to fulfill their remit regardless. However, we often find it useful to the project if the project figurehead has a keen interest in the project deliverable because it directly affects their span of control.

It is also worth considering their experience in leading business change and whether they have some knowledge of the specific business change.

Some of the personal characteristics we appreciate in an effective sponsor include assertiveness and, particularly for composite projects, emotional intelligence. This is self-awareness and ability to recognize the emotions of others and handle them sensitively and judiciously. We like sponsors who are always guided by the overall strategic goal, the *big picture*, so when the team and project manager are buried in the details of the tasks, the project remains guided by the need to achieve the benefits.

Almost all projects of any size have at least one low period. In fiction movies and novels, this scene is called, *The Dark Night of the Soul*. This is the moment the hero faces defeat but looks within to find the courage to go on toward the final conflict and climax of the story. This is when a strong sponsor that can motivate the team is invaluable. Showing the organization's leadership is behind them can make all the difference.

Project managers, of course, single-mindedly drive through the needs of the project. The sponsor can see the project in the context of the business. So, it is important the sponsor understands the project/BaU dilemma and strategically chooses the priorities throughout the project, applying pressure to obstructionist line managers or dogmatic project managers as needed.

Story: Project Sponsor Support

The following story illustrates the sort of support you can expect from a good project sponsor when a project runs into difficulties.

A large UK retail organization embarked on a project to replace its central finance system. One of the authors was engaged to manage the project after it had started. The due date had been set, but the main supplier started slowly. During the development phase, if became obvious the supplier was behind, and we had also had some issues with user acceptance testing (UAT).

Throughout, we had been reporting this component of the project as Amber to the business stakeholders. It meant that it was not a massive surprise when we asked for a meeting with the project sponsor to discuss the approval of a two month delay. From the beginning, the project sponsor had been clear that the most important output was a working system. We provided the reasons for the delay, other options, and an analysis of what we would do with the extra time. The response was agreement to a delay, a commitment to support us with senior stakeholders, and a clear message that we could only have one delay.

We could not have asked for more than that. Support alongside a firm challenge. It is always very disappointing to require a delay to the implementation of a project, but it is much easier with the right project sponsor, with the right characteristics.

Making the most of the sponsor is a key skill for a project manager. This is especially the case for composite projects.

In projects where the team is all dedicated and full time, the project manager approximates to a line manager and so encompasses similar authority. In composite projects, this is not the case; the project manager has limited positional authority over team members with as-homework staff tending to defer to their BaU manager.

The sponsor does have hierarchal authority that is recognized across departments and functions, and the project manager can acquire authority vicariously through them. A kind of reflected authority created when the sponsor convinces the team and the BaU line managers he or she is fully behind the project manager. Then, the project manager can often act as though he or she has the sponsor's authority even when the sponsor is not present.

At other times, to get the difficult things done, the project manager must use the positional authority of the sponsor directly by asking them to order it, attend the meeting, or send the e-mail.

CHAPTER 12

The Vision

More than any project, a composite project needs a clear and inspiring vision. All the best projects we have worked on have had a very clear sense of what they were about and had audacious goals.

What do we mean by a *vision*? Most projects will have a statement about the project's desired outcome, such as higher productivity. Most projects have stated outputs, which once delivered, facilitate the outcome, such as new machinery or processes. And, these usually align with business strategy. But, to really engage project teams and the people they will be working with, a statement about how everything fits together is invaluable in inspiring and guiding the team.

Why is this especially important for a composite project? A vision is good practice for any project, but in a composite project, people will be balancing the project work and their day job. Not just their time, but their mental capacity and focus will be switching into and out of the projects. A good vision helps to motivate and inspire them to keep going.

A vision emphasizes that the project is a significant event in the organization's life and should be something people want to be involved with.

If it is clear both the project and the day job are important to the business's future, it makes conversations easier by providing a common language.

The vision can inspire the business, the functional areas, and the project team to pull together, removing artificial constraints such as department boundaries and office politics.

Story: Great Latte

This story illustrates the benefit of a vision for a project, and especially a composite project.

A large UK organization embarked on a project to centralize its regional operations into a new national center in a new building. The dream was for the center to be an example to its outlets of what the company's brand stood for. This was understood in all other parts of the business, but this center was new with new processes, people, and systems. To turn the dream into something tangible, the organization engaged consultants who created a document that did just that. It described the look and feel, the tone, the expected standards within of the proposed operation, and so on.

It was much more than normal project documents like a scoping document or a business case or a design. One of the authors was engaged to run the project to open the center. The vision document was in place already, so it was great to plan the route to opening using the document as the checkpoint.

It informed the choice of everything, for example, external signage, the internal fixtures and fittings, and the uniforms for the new staff. It even specified the need for *Great Lattes* as a signal of the attention to detail and quality required of the brand. Given this brief and 500 visitors daily, the planning of how to provide coffee took us some time. It was also helpful when dealing with suppliers because it set our expectations of their products and services in a clear and tangible way.

CHAPTER 13

Team Selection

A composite project has both dedicated and as-homework team members. The dedicated staff need to be aware of the unique issues associated with composite projects and the pressures on the as-homework staff. When selecting the as-homework resources, it is important to consider whether they are going to be able to cope with the demands of the project and their day job. But it is rare for organizations to have a free hand in selection; there are always constraints. Some may have volunteered. Some may be essential because of their unique skills, knowledge, and experience, particularly domain knowledge.

Team selection tends to be a rolling top-down process, starting with the project's three key project decision makers:

- *The project sponsor* is responsible for realizing the benefits promised by the project.
- *The business lead* is responsible for the business changes, once the other project deliverables are in place. For example, if a new payment system is being introduced to reduce the cost of paying suppliers. There are workstreams to deliver the new IT system and processes, and the business lead runs the workstream to create and train the smaller payments team.
- *The project manager* is responsible for all project deliverables.

As we have said, in the agile world, the project sponsor equates to the *product owner*; the project manager equates to the *scrum master*; the workstream leads and workstream members equate to the *team members*. The business lead is responsible for business changes irrespective of the techniques used to create project outputs.

1. *The business lead* is chosen by the project sponsor from within the business. Almost always as-homework and as low as maybe half a day per week. This needs to be a manager with a direct interest in the outcome of the project, in that they are responsible for at least one of the areas affected by the project. This makes them a domain or subject matter expert (SME). They need to be credible with senior stakeholders and become a key point of contact with that group.

2. *The project manager* is chosen by the sponsor in conjunction with the business lead:
   - Could be from within the business, but more likely external.
   - Dedicated to the project, although not necessarily full time. Time likely to flex over the project life.
   - Project methodology expert, effective at tailoring, and able to flex along the way.
   - Has experience of composite projects for all the reasons we have discussed so far.
   - Strong stakeholder management skills, credible, experienced.
   - Emotionally intelligent, high level of interpersonal skills.
   - Ideally, subject matter expertise, but this is less important than the qualities listed.
   - In the next chapter, we expand on the ideal characteristics of a project manager for composite projects.

3. *The workstream leads* are chosen by the business lead and the project manager.
   These are the people project managing the sub-projects or workstreams:
   - Usually, from the business, the workstream leads need to be people with the seniority, authority, credibility, and knowledge to run a work package through a small group of people.
   - As-homework with maybe one to two days per week out of their day job.
   - Probably a volunteer.
   - The project manager should be expected to help, coach, cajole, and identify and rectify problems if the workstream goes off track.

4. *The workstream members* are selected by the project manager and the workstream leads:
   - SMEs.
   - As-homework and dedicated resources.

- Level of effort dependent on the project, but it is rarely effective unless they commit at least one day per week.
- Good process review and improvement skills.

5. *Super SME.* If the complexity of the project demands it, the business lead and the project manager may employ an overarching domain or SME:

- For some very complex projects, you may need someone who understands the end to end process in detail. It reduces the risk that the workstreams deliver incompatible solutions.
- What is important is the domain knowledge rather than hierarchal position, as this is the origin of their authority—detailed, hands-on knowledge.
- Could be two to three days per week involvement.
- Skilled at running workshops, process review, and process improvement.
- Skilled stakeholder manager. Can be involved in project board meetings to provide key knowledge when decisions are made.

Watch out for the following:

- Projects rarely have a free hand in choosing resources, as they must take staff who are available. Be aware of the risks when forced to compromise on the skills, knowledge, and experience.
- Anybody is often not better than nobody. There are people with negative productivity. People whose work must be redone or who absorb disproportionate time from the rest of the team.
- Project manager diplomatic skills are often required when business-as-usual (BaU) line managers are reluctant to let people go, and even if they do, later restrict their time on the project. Use the sponsor to pull rank if needed, but be aware you may create an enemy.
- There is often huge pressure at the start to get going. A common recruitment mistake is panicking into taking on lots of new inappropriate resource.
- Recruiting and inducting new people takes a lot of time and is a diversion from other things.
- Sometimes, removing under-performing people speeds things up. This often happens informally within sub-teams (they just stop giving the problem individual things to do). On a project

to implement a radio system for the English Channel Tunnel, one of the software engineers caused lots of rework, so he was given smaller and smaller parts to do with longer and longer timescales and then shifted to review and testing only.

Story: Direct Selling Project

The following story illustrates how, once you have categorized the project as a composite project, it is vital to reflect it in the selection and briefing of the team.

A large organization decided to move to a new method of selling its products to its business-to-business market. The method was quite common in the sector, but the organization was now ready to move and use the lessons from its competitors. This was a complex project that affected about 40 percent of the sales.

One of the authors was referred to the organization as someone with experience of composite projects and took on the management of the project. As part of the discovery phase, we identified resource gaps for the target operating model and for the project itself.

As with many companies, a fixed headcount number was imposed to control costs. The business case incorporated the operational resources, but there was limited budget for additional project resources. Also, the knowledge and expertise required meant only the operational people could support the project design and implementation.

In these circumstances, it is normally possible to backfill roles with temporary staff, but this was impractical. It would have taken too long to train the temporary staff, and we were budget- and time-constrained.

Having completed project initiation, this was clearly a composite project. The project sponsor had suspected this in time to appoint a suitably qualified project manager. We moved forward with confirming the project team members and were able to explain the need for their part-time involvement combined with their day job. This is not always palatable, but it is important to set expectations on both sides. From this point forward, we embarked on our properly diagnosed composite project though to a successful outcome.

CHAPTER 14

The Stakeholder PM

In our working lives, we have watched many project managers in action with many different styles. From the hands-on to hands-off and from the autocratic to the consultative. But, in relation to running composite projects, we think an approach on a spectrum from method-driven to stakeholder-driven is the most useful.

The *method-driven* project manager was summed up in the prologue project story by the character Matt Mefford. Matt's experience and background were IT starting as a business analyst, but it could have been a coder, and a natural career progression led him into project management. Other typical backgrounds are construction or engineering. Such PMs are typically familiar with projects organized with dedicated, full-time resources.

The Method-Driven Project Manager

Method-driven PMs are also found with backgrounds in business who, as a middle-managers, realized they were good at delivering projects and so made the switch. They will have done Level 1 and Level 3 projects comfortably and some Level 2 composite projects, but unrecognized as such, and so found them annoying and problematic.

On paper, these PMs look very promising candidates. They have worked with people up and down, and across the organization and covered multiple functional areas in the organization. The contractors and consultants among them will have covered multiple functional areas and worked in many different organizations.

They will have formal qualifications, usually college graduates, occasionally a second degree (MSc, MBA), plus certification in PRINCE2, APM, PMI, or equivalent, and have a strong skill set:

- Can manage the full project lifecycle.
- Project team creation.
- Project plan development.
- Formal stakeholder management and communication plan creations.
- Very capable with office products—Outlook, Word, Excel, PowerPoint, and PM software tools such as MS Project.
- Subject matter expertise from their previous life, like IT or construction.

They tend to have the personal attributes or personality to *get the job done*:

- Very organized.
- Tenacious.
- Rigorous and pay attention to detail.
- Method-driven and adhere to the process. Expect this of everyone else too.
- Adherent to organizational governance.
- Task-focused and have the attitude that "it isn't a popularity contest, I'm here to get it done," so, frequently annoys and upsets members of the team and beyond to drive the project to conclusion.

When working on composite projects, there are risks with method-driven PMs. Indifferent or intolerant to the pressures and limited time of the as-homework staff and so there is high chance of conflict, anger, and aggression. Meetings that spill over into frustration and finger pointing. They may use *naming and shaming* of slippage offenders because they will not accept the day job sometimes has to come first.

The Stakeholder-Driven Project Manager

On the other end of the spectrum is what we call the *stakeholder-driven* project manager.

The method-driven PM is focused and skilled at the hard skills of project management: the methodology, process, and tools. By contrast, the stakeholder-driven project manager has those skills and, in addition, puts a lot of time on the soft skills of project management. In particular, the relationships and understanding of the stakeholders, the people involved and impacted by the project.

This is a gross generalization, but the stakeholder-driven PM is less likely to come from a traditional projectized sector like IT, engineering, or construction. Instead, they are more likely from a business manager background. They are likely to have managed a business-as-usual (BaU) team with a profit-responsible or customer-facing role. This route means they are likely to have experienced composite projects as the norm and probably had their first experiences of the phenomenon from the other side, as a manager releasing staff to a composite project. Their first experience on a project was probably as a workstream lead or subject matter expert on a composite project. When they were given their first project manager role, they were probably running a team of people who had BaU responsibilities.

These managers generally have project management certifications and other business or professional qualifications.

In addition to the skills mentioned for the method-driven PM, the stakeholder-driven PM is commercially aware, allowing them to relate to the senior management team and line managers of the departments impacted by the project. However, the key additional skill they bring is a developed emotional intelligence. That is, they are aware of, in control of, and able to express their emotions and to handle interpersonal relationships wisely and empathetically. They bring this to bear in the large amount of communication, persuasion, and negotiation needed during a composite project.

In terms of stakeholder management, they can see beyond the obvious stakeholders to the wider impact. For example, the project team member's line managers who may be reluctant to allow their people to work on the project; or the personal assistants who can have impact and influence beyond what their position in the hierarchy might suggest, and who often ensure the organization ticks along.

They tend to have the personal attributes to combine management and leadership:

- Very organized.
- Tenaciously firm but fair. Knowing when to press hard, guided by an awareness of what can be allowed to slip as a trade-off against a team member's day jobs.
- Rigorous and pay attention to detail but also able to see the big picture and so able to summarize, consolidate up in reports, and communicate in a way that key messages are heard and acted on.
- Emotionally intelligent with an understanding about what makes people *tick* and how to get the best out of them. They have strong interpersonal skills.
- Builds working relationships very quickly.
- Perceived to have credibility, calmness, and gravitas.

How does the approach differ?

- Unlike method-driven PMs who rigorously follow the methodology, the stakeholder-driven PM is adept at tailoring the method. They adapt the method to match the complexity, criticality, and scale of the project. Importantly, they adapt to meet the needs of BaU and the team members' familiarity with the method. This is likely to be seen as risky by senior managers, and the PM needs superior negotiation skills to achieve.
- There may be conflict with stakeholders, but only if absolutely necessary and on purpose.
- May challenge organizational governance, for example, to bypass certain processes to ensure the project and the business can co-exist. Again, the PM will likely have to negotiate with skeptical senior managers.
- Clear focus on the project outcomes, always thinking ahead, with clear understanding of constraints, and how to eliminate them.

Table 14.1 summarizes some of the characteristics described:

Table 14.1 Comparison of method- and stakeholder-driven project managers

Method driven	Stakeholder driven
Slave to the methodology	Master of the methodology
Methodology focused, tools and techniques	Methodology flexible, makes methodology work for them
Process aware	Commercially aware
Hard skills	Soft skills
Tool driven	People focused
Stakeholder by rote	Stakeholder sensitive
Rigid	Flexible
Linear	Rounded
Black and white	Technicolour
	Emotionally intelligent
	Stakeholder intelligent
	Empathetic
Says no	Says no in a way the customer thinks is a yes
Deliver at all costs	May compromise on delivery but leaves people in tact
Governance junky	Appropriate rigour
Hired gun	Trusted advisor
Accepts the strategy	Challenges the strategy

Story: The Right Project Manager

The following story illustrates that many organizations do understand the need for the right project manager, when kicking off a composite project.

A large U.K. organization, which was a specialist in providing operational services, won a contract with a new customer. The customer's expectation was, rightly, that the day-to-day operation was not to be affected by the start of the new contract. The timing of the win was out of step with their resource plan, so they required short notice external support.

The organization was an existing customer of one of the authors. The text said "Hi. Do you have two days per week for six weeks? We have won a contract—couldn't say anything till now. We need your support to help the team implement the service. Cheers John." We replied, "I don't, but I know a man that can."

Having worked together many times, we both knew this was a composite project. The operations team would have to run their day jobs as well as provide subject matter expertise on the transition project. Their time and availability would be precious. The project manager would have to be great in front of their customer.

That was Friday. On Monday at 8.30 a.m., we were with the team with Peter. John trusted me to the point there was no need for any real assessment of Peter.

Why? That sounds a bit risky.

There were two reasons.

Firstly, Peter would be working under the author's commercial umbrella as an approved supplier. Secondly, and more importantly, John knew the author would bring someone along who was a black belt in composite project management. He would be great with the stakeholders in John's business and with customers.

The transition was successful, and Peter really enjoyed working with the team and they really enjoyed working with him.

CHAPTER 15

Start Right

Ensuring the project is set up well is important for all projects. It is particularly important for projects using team members who spend most of their lives in business as usual (BaU) and are doing the project as-homework.

Building a Team from the Project Members

We covered team selection earlier, but once that is in place, the next step is to introduce the project manager, business lead, and project sponsor to the project members, and then meld those individuals into a team. With an all full-time dedicated group, this often happens naturally. Bruce Tuckman's model[1] for this is shown in Figure 15.1, as new people come together, there are personality conflicts, competition for influence, and communication difficulties due to different assumptions and outlooks. Through necessity, disagreements are resolved with accommodations and compromises, and misunderstandings are cleared up. This leads to increasing effectiveness as the group starts to function as a team. Effectiveness is accelerated as the team builds trust and increasingly works to each other's strengths.

However, this process may not happen naturally and particularly for part-time members who regularly go back to the comfort of their normal BaU team. You may have to coach transition through the stages.

A key tool is to build a shared understanding of the project's vision, with the project team. This is achieved via the kick-off workshop, meetings with workstream leaders and members, and so on. This is useful to hold the team together and to drive the project forward. When difficulties arise and heads drop and shoulders droop, raise them by getting them to look up at the inspiring vision they emotionally committed to.

---

[1] Bonebright, D.A. 2010. "40 years of Storming: A Historical Review of Tuckman's Model of Small Group Development." *Human Resource Development International* 13, no. 1.

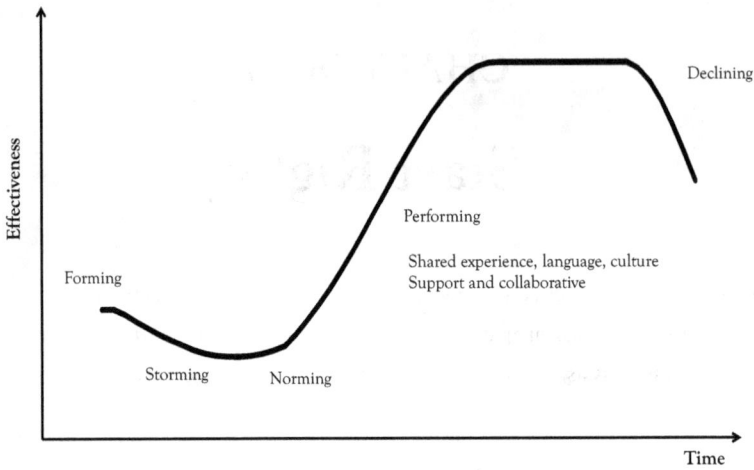

Figure 15.1 Tuckman's stages of team development

A *buzz* of being part of something important motivates. So, another useful tool to enhance morale is promotion of the project and the project team throughout the business. After the staff know about the project, the next interest is who is going to be doing it and so, the announcement of the team to the business can be used to promote the project and motivate the team members.

A complication for team dynamics is movement of people into and out of the team. This may be planned due to the changing project resource requirements or unplanned and forced by external events. Do not just assume a new team member will be easily assimilated. Plan for their arrival, induct them into the environment, and monitor they are positive and not disruptive to the smooth functioning of the team.

Understand Your Team

If you did not pick the team, spend time to understand the people and the way they work. They will be driven by attitude, aspirations, and fears, so you will not likely have total support and compliance. Has their past work and experience prepared them for any of the tasks on this project?

Consider having the team complete Myers–Briggs[2] tests for them and you to learn how they may best perform as a team member.

---

[2]   See Myers-Briggs Foundation, https://myersbriggs.org

This will help you build a sense of working as a team and not as individuals. If you make sure everyone understands how others depend on their output, you can instill a sense of *not letting the team down*.

Project Methodology

Do not overcomplicate things.

Project methodology, processes, and documents are there to help projects run smoothly and not act as a straitjacket. Formal structured methodologies and project management tools can be complex and frustrating for anyone not familiar with them. In some cases, there may even be a blend of techniques in play. For example, a workstream could be using agile principles to create software, while PRINCE2 is used in the construction workstream. The inexperienced or unsure project manager defaults to rigid adherence to the methodology. The PM who really understands the method and the purpose of each process and output can skillfully tailor the project documentation to the needs of the project, the business, and the people involved. Find a reasonable and workable compromise.

As-homework team members are unlikely to be intimately familiar with the documents and tools, so adapt and simplify as much as feasible. Aim for one-page documents such as *plan on a page* and *status report on a page*. Take the time to make documents clear and concise so that they can be reviewed by busy people in a few minutes. Even then, do not assume the message has been received and understood. If you need to communicate serious issues, then the best methods are a phone call or face-to-face.

Part of adapting the project environment is making it as familiar to the people as possible. Use terminology common to that business. Use existing forms of communication in expected formats such as visual boards and existing intranets. Tap into existing meeting structures such as weekly management meetings for quick updates. Use familiar surroundings such as nearby meeting rooms and war rooms.

Do not make the mistake of overestimating the project management knowledge of the as-homework staff. Team members may be reluctant to admit they do not understand the terminology or methodology, but equally, you do not want to patronize them. Make an informal assessment of their project knowledge during discussions and then, where necessary, educate the team. Your best opportunities for this are during early one-to-ones and during the kick-off and earlier-stage workshops.

If there is a project management office (PMO) function, then consult them, as they may require things to be done in a certain way and may be able to offer support in some areas. Do not be averse to challenging the PMO rules to avoid adding a level of difficulty with potentially little real project benefit.

Story: Rigorous Start up with a Sound Business Case

This story illustrates the vital importance of ensuring the projects starts on a sound basis with a strong business case.

The business was involved in supplying outside broadcast services to TV companies.

Although predictable, the company had a highly variable demand for its services both across the week and across the year. Staff worked an annual hours contract, with hours being called off anytime across the year. They were also supplemented by a significant number of freelancers.

We undertook a review of its business processes and, in particular, its employment model in considering moving a large part of its staff to freelance status. Freelance rates were apparently favorable, and savings were to be had from avoiding the generous pension contribution, but there were redundancy costs (different for each person) to be considered.

With such complicated business and employment processes, they needed a sophisticated financial model to determine the value and impact of the proposed changes under varying demand growth assumptions.

To general surprise, the model revealed a long payback period and a poor return on investment for the switch. This meant that the management were able to avoid a costly and disruptive change to the business.

Initiation

In this section, we list out the steps we take so that a composite project is setup to succeed. It is intended to act as a checklist focused on the things specifically for composite projects:

- Have a kick-off workshop event to set the stage. The goals are for everyone to get to know each other, create a collective vision for the project to focus minds and boost morale, brainstorm the deliverables, and explore the risks.
- Project initiation document (PID). The PID may be a single document or more often collection of documents that defines the why, what, when, and who. Next, we focus on the aspects vital for a composite project:
  - The project manager creates the PID, but it should be issued by the project sponsor. As a person with hierarchal authority and reputation, this means it will register with people even if it is not read.
  - The document explains what the project is all about, but do not assume the message has been received. To confirm all the key stakeholders have understood and support the initiative, it is necessary to meet face-to-face one-to-one or with small groups. This ensures attention but, as importantly, allows you to gauge response, understanding, and commitment.
  - Sometimes, for a contentious project, it is worth having people physically sign the document. This can sometimes be brought out later in a formal way to reinstate commitments that have lapsed, but just the act of signing creates an internal strong commitment in people. The act of signing has strong cultural significance in our society that you can use.
  - Dwight D. Eisenhower said, "Plans are worthless, but planning is everything." We certainly do not go that far, but we do endorse the sentiment that the benefit of the PID is not only the output document, but also the process of working together and the thinking that it forces on the team.

- Scope. It is vital everyone knows what is going to be involved:
  - ○ Only then can as-homework members have any idea they have the capacity to deliver the project.
  - ○ It is also a vital tool in managing scope creep. It is inevitable that calls to add more better features will arise. A loose ambiguous scope definition leaves you exposed. By contrast, a tight explicit scope definition, along with the concepts of the project triangle and people project triangle, allows you to ensure the impacts are understood by the project board. In particular, the usual problem of the pressure on the as-homework staff is not overlooked. Your argument for properly resourcing any scope extension can be well evidenced.
- Project team and responsibilities. Without this, it is impossible to commit to delivery or to determine how much time each person must devote to the project. Again, it is the as-homework staff that are most vulnerable and so most in need of clarity as to responsibilities.
- Assumptions, constraints, and dependencies.
  - ○ A plan is about the future, and the future is uncertain. Rather than give up in the face of uncertainty, it is necessary to make educated estimates and forecasts and plan on that basis. However, ensure everyone agrees those assumptions are realistic.
  - ○ Publicizing how each person's output affects others—dependencies—especially on the critical path, is a great help to as-homework people who struggle to see far enough ahead to make those connections. A key role of the PM is to know which tasks to push and what can be allowed to slip and so sparing pressure on as-homework staff if possible.
- Communications plan. A plan of what information and what messages, to whom, by what media, and how often. The as-homework staff and their BaU managers need careful consideration, more on that later.
- Detailed plan.
  - ○ Obviously, this is vital for the PM, but the process of creating this by workshopping it is of immense value in

motivating and gaining commitment from as-homework staff who might be unfamiliar with the process. Start with the end in mind and focus on final and intermediate deliverables (product-based planning), as that is what people can envisage, and it is critical for people to see what the state will be at the end of each phase.

○ Be realistic. The well-known expression "No plan survives contact with the enemy" is true for most projects and is one of the challenges that led to the development of agile principles. The fourth agile value is "Responding to Change over following a plan."

○ Help as-homework staff by making each deliverable small. A workstream responsible for a software output will be doing this if they are using agile principles. Large complex tasks are less likely to be done because they appear daunting and cannot be done without planning. So, do not expect the staff to sub-divide their own work, do it for them. Make deadlines more frequent and more achievable. It is good for their sense of accomplishment and morale and is good for the PM in identifying slippage early.

- Initial risk assessment. Composite projects have risks unique to this kind of project, namely the interaction of the project workload with the demands of BaU. This depends on the nature of the BaU work and how predictable it is. Is the BaU customer demand and variety of the output unstable or unpredictable? If so, this will mean as-homework staff are uncertain what demands will be made on them by BaU at any time in the future.

- Apply lessons learned from other projects.
  - Our experience with business projects is that this is the worst-documented aspect of a project. If the material exists, it is very valuable; if not, it is often worth investing some time to talk to participants on similar past projects.
  - The issues on past projects are frequently symptomatic of the way an organization works. It is then very helpful to

run the team through lessons learned, or alternatively, learn
some lessons from the problems experienced.
- Mini PIDs.
  - The concept of a *mini PID* is to provide workstream PIDs.
    These documents are much shorter than the main PID,
    but require the PM and the workstream lead go through
    the same initiation thought process.

Story: Rigorous Initiation in Product Development

The following story illustrates how a sound initiation process can stop
poorly thought through projects moving to implementation.

An organization was launching several products to increase sales in its
customer service business. Given the scale of the activity, the organization required some experienced support to manage the process of
selecting and implementing a suite of products.

One of the authors was engaged to support a team establishing a
program of product developments. The team supported the franchise
network and was charged with improving service revenues and customer
satisfaction. There were several pilot products, so it was important that
they were implemented properly to test the sales and service impact.

The key activity was a rigorous initiation process to ensure each
implementation had been properly thought through and planned. We
ran workshops for each product and, together, created mini business
cases and short PIDs. This ensured we had a consistent method, and
that we asked ourselves all the difficult but necessary questions. We
were able to plug any gaps and identify risks before we started and
before we committed effort and cost.

Several projects were unable to meet the criteria we agreed. This
was a disappointment to the enthusiastic proposers, but the organization was better off not continuing projects with high risk of failure.

We created a simple review and reporting structure appropriate to
the scale of the program to monitor the implementation stage.

The products that made it through this process were all implemented in full, or as pilots, during the year as planned. It re-empha-
sized the value of the project initiation process, even for small projects.

A rigorous initiation can sometimes be used after a project has been initiated, if that makes sense. In business, sometimes, moving quickly to grab an opportunity is a sound strategy when you know you can retrofit the project governance, provided that, too, is done very swiftly. We do not think it is something we would advocate as normal practice, but we have been engaged to do this from time to time, and it has been successful.

Story: Clarity of Objectives

The following story illustrates how clear, unambiguous objectives are vital to gain support of key business stakeholders, even if those objectives are uncomfortable.

An organization operating in the public sector embarked on a reorganization that included most departments. Their brief was fluid and affected by government policy, so their team was under constant review. They had to periodically bring in new skills, move staff into different roles, and in some cases, let them go.

One of the authors supported the organization over a 10-year period and four of the reorganizations. Each time, we spent the correct amount of time to prepare the project, the organizational proposals, consultations, and so on. However, the most valuable part of the preparation was the frank conversation to agree on the objectives.

There were always very difficult decisions to make. The impact of these decisions would have a serious and unexpected impact on staff members. We found that it was vital, within the project team, to fully understand what we were trying to achieve, even if some of the objectives were very uncomfortable.

Communicating to the staff during a reorganization is tough anyway, but clarity of purpose reduces the risk of messages being misconstrued.

CHAPTER 16

Involving People Effectively

If project members lack commitment, then meeting attendance will be poor, deliverables late or incomplete, and people will start to delegate their responsibilities to others. As-homework staff always have a ready, at-hand, justification of day job commitments.

To avoid this, you need to generate visible enthusiasm. Then, you will have people exceeding expectations, making suggestions, and prepared to take on additional work. The key is to fully involve all the team and all the stakeholders with active communication geared to their needs. They will be inspired if they think they are making an important contribution to a project important to the organization's leadership. They will be inspired if the vision for the project is something they can believe in.

The kind of projects that command the most excitement are ones that look like they will succeed. The ones that look like they will succeed are backed by senior management and are self-confident in what they are about, what they will achieve, and what they want from the staff. This requires great communication. The key principles of communication are:

- Listen.
- Communicate often and honestly.
- Know your audience.
- Chose time and method.
- Confirm you have been understood.

Project Sponsor

Earlier we talked about leveraging the hierarchical power and credibility of the sponsor. Communications from the sponsor represent communication from the highest level and so commands the greatest attention.

Use the sponsor to communicate to people for whom the project is not their focus. It is critical they understand the reasons for the project and its importance, why they are involved, why specific other people are involved or not involved. They need to know how much time will be expected from them, whether it is in their objectives, and what support they will receive.

BaU Managers

Because they are not directly involved in the project, it is easy to overlook the crucial communication needs for the BaU managers of the project team members. The communications goal for them is to encourage them to be supportive of a project that does not directly help them, but may inconvenience or even make life hard for them. You want them to be happy to release their people to the project and to remain supportive if BaU has unexpected needs or if the project has additional unexpected needs. It is vital they understand the importance of the project and feel involved and contributing to its success.

Let them join in and celebrate milestones achieved and help them feel they are contributing to that success. Then, if problems arise, they may have some ownership and be disposed to contribute more to bring the project back on track.

One of the most powerful techniques for winning over BaU managers are one-to-one meetings where the PM mostly listens. You can make more friends in a morning by becoming interested in the BaU managers than you ever will by trying to get the BaU managers interested in you and your project. To put it another way, taking from Stephen Covey,[1] seek first to understand, then to be understood. What is it you will understand? Meetings like this allow you to plan the project around BaU cycles such as identifying the optimum time to go live or other key events. They help you plan resource availability around month end, year-end, product launches, other BaU-critical periods. This may extend the delivery of the project, and that is a case to argue with the project board. These meetings

---

[1] Covey, S. 2013. *Seven Habits of Highly Successful People*. Simon and Schuster UK; Reissue Edition.

are also where you start to understand BaU-related project risks and business risks.

Communications at Launch of the Project

The best opportunity to set the tone is at the beginning, at the project announcement, and at the PID launch.

Ongoing Communications

Carefully plan what information and what messages, to whom, when, by what media, and how often.

You need to carefully consider what the as-homework staff need. Provide too much information they do not regard as relevant and they will start to ignore all communications, missing the crucial messages you need them to see. However, provide not enough information, and they will feel excluded and not a full part of the project, especially if they are spending most of their time away in BaU. This is a matter of judgment of the individuals and the culture. Try a plan and then seek feedback on how well it is working. Then, adjust as appropriate.

Communicate Often and Honestly

Lack of truth in reporting is found out and destroys trust. It follows that you should deliver bad news as early as possible. This ensures the business has its expectations under control and enables help to be sought while things are repairable.

In other words, avoid giving the impression all is well and then spring imminent disaster on the business when it is too late for anyone to help. To borrow from another consultant, avoid reporting, "Green, green, green, train crash."

Story: Communication Is Vital

The following story illustrates how the design and delivery of a good communications plan can keep the business comfortable with the project and avoid *ad hoc* questions and request for information.

A large retail organization had a weekly reporting cycle for its retail outlets to report sales, stock, and so on. They decided to change the day of the week on which the outlets were expected to report. Given its impact on statutory and shareholder reporting requirements, the change could only be made at year end.

One of the authors was engaged to manage the project. The change affected 50 systems and 650 outlets and was reliant on the commitment of several stakeholder groups. This included the outlet managers who had to amend their working practices and stock taking routines.

A small team worked for three months to prepare and communicate the switchover. The change was carried out over the weekend of the financial year end. The key activity over the weekend was frequent monitoring with a follow up system for outlets that were behind schedule.

The exercise was successfully completed as planned and on time. There were three reasons:

1. A fixed implementation date helps focus the minds of everybody on the project.
2. The excellent and intensive communication by the operational team to the outlets before and during the change.
3. A tool was designed to make it simple easy for the busy outlet managers to report progress against the go-live milestones.

CHAPTER 17

Dealing with People Day to Day

Running the Plan

You have tailored the methodology to match the organization and team culture and experience. You have created a workable plan and communicated a clear critical path and dependencies. The resource plan is realistic and assumes less time will be available than the managers and individuals have committed to. On top if this, you have project manager contingency. Now, you must manage the plan.

This means monitoring progress and taking control actions to remove barriers or respond to missed or poor deliverables. For an agile output, this will be at the daily standup meetings where the team focuses on tasks done, in progress, and to be done.

Manage the plan sensibly and sensitively, push tasks on the critical path, be more relaxed where slippage can occur. The art of running composite projects is knowing when as-homework staff can be pushed.

Never assume the project will have the time it needs from as-homework staff, and you may need to establish agreements on the use of their time. Fortunately, your project plan has lots of small frequent deliverables, so you have a clear accurate view of progress and always have time to make adjustments.

Fend off scope creep like your job depends on it, because it does. Fortunately, your unambiguous deliverables' definition and your understanding of the people's project triangle help you manage expectations on these issues.

Similarly, resist attempts to bring deadlines forward—it is never going to work. Our experience is that enough unanticipated events happen and cause all the disruption and challenges to scope and deadlines you can deal with, without adding more.

Meetings

Meetings are vital, and if used well, can achieve a lot. But, everybody has experienced inefficient and ineffective meetings, and everyone hates that type. Meetings fail if they are perceived as irrelevant for too many people for too much of the meeting time. Too many failed meetings and the project can be in jeopardy.

You need to make it as easy as possible for people to meet your expectations. The key is to respect everyone's time. This means tailoring meetings to the needs of the project, the business, and the people involved. Work around busy times in the day, week, month, and year. Where possible, fit into the rhythm of the business by using existing reporting cycles and *piggyback* on existing meetings.

Aim for short meetings regularly, rather than long meetings, and remember not everyone has to attend every meeting for all the time. Think about using the agile approach to meetings—quick fire stand-up meetings to review progress and agree the plan for today and tomorrow. Consider sub-dividing the team around common interests or design the agenda to ensure maximum participation and engagement. A lot can be efficiently achieved with project manager one-to-one meetings with workstream leaders. In general, whole team meetings should be infrequent, but are sometimes appropriate with a small team.

As not everyone will find everything important, allow people to join just relevant parts of the meeting. Allowing people to join meetings remotely—this reduces travel overhead and aids productivity but must be managed well. There are considerable risks unless the meeting chair is considerate to the remote participants. The chair must ensure they are following the discussion, and they are able to contribute.

Another tip is to book in meetings right at the start for the duration of the project. This way, they are recorded into people's diaries and are factored into their plans for subsequent weeks and months.

To make meetings as effective as possible, have a clear purpose and agenda with a logical sequence of topics that lead to outcomes.

This allows attendees to prepare themselves and leave feeling something has been accomplished.

Meeting rules that are outside the organization norms are extremely difficult to impose. So, you might think that *no laptops* and *phones off* will improve the effectiveness of the meeting, and you are probably right. However, if in all other company meetings, attendees routinely check e-mails and take calls, then you are almost certainly going to have to accept it, because the lost goodwill is rarely going to be worth it. Choose your battles.

However, you can:

- Start on time.
- When you have a group together, use the time for discussion rather than wasting it battling through the plan or risk logs.
- Efficient use of time is to focus on deviations from the plan—exception management. Time, cost, and quality have tolerances, so only if these are exceeded are they important. Risks that have changed status are relevant.
- Minute the project boards and project team meetings. Focus on updates, plus decisions and actions.
- Issue the minutes within 24 hours so that people with actions are not delayed from starting and when it is still fresh in their minds.

Minutes can be the primary tool to chase actions in between meetings rather than using project status meetings to embarrass people with delinquent statuses. Ensure they know they are amber before the meetings.

For non-attendees, then BaU has probably interfered and you need to be patient. Having follow-up contact with people who were not able to attend shows you recognize their issues and puts the project in the front of their mind again.

Reports

The same principle of respecting people's time applies to reports. All reports should be concise and focused on exceptions to the plan. This means they take minimal time to read and only contain relevant actionable information.

If workstream leaders are reporting, provide them with templates so that they can focus on content and not structure, are common across the project, take minimal time to write and read. If available, use in-house reporting tools that focus on efficiency for report writing.

Story: Believable Reporting

The following story illustrates how believable reporting of program or project status builds belief within the project and team and senior stakeholders.

A large UK organization embarked on a project to:

1. Add built capacity to its head office, including extra training rooms and more shared space.
2. Relocate another operation sharing the site to a new place.
3. Deliver a package of smaller refurbishments.
4. Ensure the existing operation was not affected.

One of the authors was engaged to manage the project. This was an additional project with an existing customer and so, we were known quantities for each other. This program ran for 12 months and was reported as green for the entire duration. There were, of course, issues that cropped up during the project, but none predicted to affect the budget or opening day.

This contrasted with the other project we were running, at the same time, with the same customer, which was rather more problematic and spent quite a bit of time at amber and even red at some points. It is vital to report accurately, even it is uncomfortable. It is part of the journey to obtaining support to bring your project back to green and build a level of trust with stakeholders.

In the case of the head office program, the Green throughout was only credible because the author was not afraid to report very truthfully on other projects and prepared to take the short-term pain with stakeholders by going amber or red if required.

Fortunately and with a great deal of effort from the project team, the program was delivered in time and on budget.

Tackle the Day Job Issue

You cannot escape the day job issue; it has to be tackled. It is always easy for the day job to take precedence for reasons already discussed: it has frequent deadlines; their line manager holds hierarchal authority not the PM; day job tasks can seem more urgent and immediate; the day job may simply be easier as it is more familiar.

People tend to mistake urgent for important, so working through that confusion helps staff reprioritize. However, the project manager must accept the reality of composite projects, in that there will be conflicts between the project and day job. The day job is a genuine excuse for lack of work, and it is likely to be so frequently.

Get to know the team, understand their individual BaU pressures, not just at the start, but as the project progresses. Understand their background and motivations: are they are volunteers or conscripts, is the project part of their objectives? The use of annual objectives for the project team can help project and BaU work have similar weight.

Do not forget the motivational power of being listened to and of recognition of effort and achievement:

- Have one-to-one meetings for workstream leaders and other team members to provide this.
- Use of the usual company *treats*—meeting biscuits, small rewards—is symbolic, but often effective.
- Encourage the sponsor to give recognition to the team.
- Use a mid-project or post-project *jolly* or bonuses as appropriate to company culture.

The project manager must ensure the day job is not the easy option and the project the difficult one:

- Make project processes as easy to follow as possible.
- Assign small, frequent deliverables.
- Coordinate project demands with BaU peak demands.
- Have strong relationships with BaU line managers.
- Communicate strong sponsor backing to the BaU managers.

- Create a team spirit so that missing deadlines is letting down real-life colleagues rather than just an intangible ephemeral project.
- Have formal time commitment agreements in place.
- Always follow up on missed expectations, such as missed meetings and missed deadlines.
- Be prepared to use a line manager or sponsor to escalate. Sometimes, you need to just use the positional authority of executive sponsor to get the difficult things done.

What this means is be human and empathetic while keeping clear focus on the end goal.

Story: Simplify with Project Management

The following story illustrates how a complex problem can be broken down into something that is deliverable using good project management.

A large UK organization, which was a specialist in providing operational services, won a tender to manage bad weather resilience for a transport hub. They were the lead contractor, bringing together a standby team drawn from their team, other supplier resource and customer headcount. The scale was such that the solution designed was very complex.

As you might expect, the resilience solution was designed to stand by 24 hours a day at times of forecast bad weather. Desk-based simulations were performed to understand the snow clearing requirements for certain snow conditions. The resource requirements were calculated, and the numbers were very large.

The complexity here was the solution itself. Therefore, the approach had to be like the old quotation—"How do you eat an elephant? One bite at a time."

The risk here was that the scale of the analysis, training, and rostering would prove too daunting to the subject matter experts, and they would find a way to avoid the project. The skill required was to break the task down into manageable slices that would enable use of the precious time of the operational experts. Also, to engage all stakeholders to ensure they all understood the reputational benefits to the organization of making this work. The next stage was to very carefully plan meetings, attendees, agendas, and so on. This strategy worked to the extent we were able to be ready for action as the worst weather hit.

CHAPTER 18

Get the Important Stuff Done

Project management can be a maelstrom of activity and events. These events emanate from inside and outside the project. They relate to every level of the project like a high-level strategic partner taking a change of direction to a personal crisis of a team member. Most of the issues are detail and can be a fog, clouding the critical problems and distracting from important tasks that must be delivered.

Overall success is most likely to be achieved if the sponsor and project manager are clear what the vital deliveries are and what they depend on. They communicate this to the team, and priority goes to the right things, sacrificing what can be lost and delaying what can be delivered late.

Use the project triangle and people project triangle to understand and communicate trade-offs, but in general, business projects are judged successful if they work, even if slightly over budget, and the scope has had to be massaged.

Story: The Prototype

The following story illustrates how, once you have categorized the project as a composite project, it is possible to deploy tactics to short-cut the work for the project team.

A UK organization decided to overhaul the contract it had in place with its franchisees. The reason was to reflect new and upcoming changes in their marketplace and to the products they sold.

The organization requested one of the authors to update the standards section of the proposed contract. For reasons of resource pressure, they were behind their own schedule for publishing to their franchisees. In this case, the requirement for support was for both project support and sector expertise.

Each of the standards had a business owner who was accountable for signing off *their* section. The importer was at a very busy time for several reasons. The subject matter experts (SMEs) were flat out, and we figured out that to meet them, update the documents and then meet them again for signoff would have taken much longer than we had.

To minimize the time required from the SMEs, we created a prototype for the standards, using multiple existing sources of information, our operational knowledge, and understanding of the sector. This provided a draft document to review, rather than a clean sheet of paper. It is referred to as an *Aunt Sally* or a *starter for 10*. It showed that we knew what we were talking about, which in turn, built trust. This meant the SMEs were happy to brief us on the changes and be confident that their guidelines would be accurate without too much further input from them.

Using this method and prioritizing the important tasks, we were able to meet the deadline for delivery of the contractual documents to the franchisees.

CHAPTER 19

Summary

This has been a practical book advocating a particular approach for a particular type of business project that changes the way business-as-usual is done.

The modern business environment is one of rapid change. The modern corporation is lean and very cost conscious. A consequence is an increasingly common project management situation of a medium important, medium complex business change project that cannot justify a full-time team. Instead, these projects are staffed by in-house resources working on the project in addition to their normal responsibilities. We term these as-homework staff, and the projects, composite projects.

The thesis of the book is that:

1. Composite projects are being used at an increasing rate to meet the demands of rapid business change.
2. They are largely unrecognized as a separate organizational category of project with particular characteristics, management needs, and risks.
3. We maintain that there is a people project triangle with trade-off between the project, ongoing business, and people working in both the business and the project. When pressure mounts, generally, only two of those can be prioritized, and one must give. We observe that it is often the people who bear the brunt with subsequence implications of stress, burnout, and damaged reputations.
4. However, with better recognition, clearer understanding, and appropriate measures, many of the common problems with composite projects can be foreseen and mitigated or avoided, and we have provided our suggestions.

We provided a framework for identifying when composite projects can be used. Then, a series of chapters recommending practical techniques and approaches for dealing with the issues specific to composite projects.

The Right Approach

The right approach is a mentality of stakeholder-driven rather than methodology-driven. The stakeholder-driven project manager understands projects are done by people and impact other people such as the managers of the as-homework project staff. Consequently, they develop soft skills concerning understanding people and relationships in addition to the methodology project management skills.

Effective and Effective Use of the Sponsor Is Key

Leverage the hierarchical power and credibility of the sponsor to secure budget, free up resources, and focus project teams. Use them in communications to affect the greatest attention.

Understand the Team

The project needs to be done by the project staff, so understanding the individuals is vital: their motivations, skills, limitations, including those imposed by their BaU managers.

Realize that the BaU managers, although not in the team, can have a major impact on the project. So, understand them and their issues, involve them, and help them to feel engaged and contributing to the project success.

Do not expect the group to be effective automatically. They need to be forged into a team. Start by inspiring them with a vision of the positive change the project will deliver.

Respect People's Time

Time is the key scarce resource of as-homework staff, so do not squander it.

Communication

Plan and tailor as-homework staff communication for them. Use media and language appropriate for them. Communicate frequently and succinctly. Do not alienate them with information they do not need and are not interested in; otherwise, they will ignore it and miss vital information. Make further information available for them if they are interested.

Have effective and efficient meetings: appropriate size, attendees, agenda, allow part and remote attendance.

Methodology

Keep things simple, adapt the methodology for the skill levels and time limitations of your team. Make it easy for staff, do not expect them to sub-divide their work. Instead, issue small frequent deliverables.

The Day Job

Be keenly aware of the day job pressures, not in general terms, but specifically. This allows you, where possible, to plan the project around them. Also, be very clear of the project dependencies so that you can know when and what to flex and still meet critical timescales.

---

1. Right approach
   - Stakeholder driven rather than methodology driven
2. Effective and effective use of the sponsor is key
3. Understand the team
   - Inspire them with the vision
   - Don't expect the group to automatically be a team
   - They have BaU managers—involve them
4. Respect people's time
   - Concise as-homework staff communication and efficient meetings
   - Keep things simple—adapt methodology
   - Make it easy with small frequent deliverables
   - Tackle the day job issue
   - Know when and what to flex and timescales

Figure 19.1 Summary of advice specifically for composite projects

However, sometimes, the day job issue must be confronted and time on the project preserved. This is another time the sponsor might be key.

Finally

These recommendations based on our experience are summarized in Figure 19.1. We hope that this book can start a debate about the nature and specific problems of composite projects. We look forward to hearing other people's research and experience and adding them to our toolkit.

Epilogue

You will remember Project Kark Rash from the Prologue; here's the same project but using much of the learning from this book.

Project Sub Lime

Jake Holder, a project manager at Nat Retail Brands Limited (NRB) and responsible for the new Single Training Center (STC) operational launch, again looked anxiously at his watch. In less than an hour, he would have to face Malcolm Shots, the CEO, and he had no idea what he was going to tell him.

They had launched on time, but it was a slightly cut back launch, but it certainly had the *wow factor* wanted by the CEO. The first delegate survey was good; also, he looked again at the project finance report telling him he was within acceptable tolerance of less than five percent over budget. He knew the marketing director was surprised the opening had not affected the quarterly marketing reports. The site director also managed to re-locate five stores using some of the STC project team.

He also suspected one of his project team, who happened to know Malcolm socially from the golf club, may have had a slightly different view of the project.

There had been the inevitable teething troubles, but the resource plan and the enthusiasm of the team ensured they were resolved quickly. Nothing systemic was wrong, and all the stakeholders were briefed to expect some short-term issues.

He did not think anything had gone wrong. He had tailored the company's project management method to the specific needs of the project. He had insisted the project board was extended to include the key stakeholders.

He had worked hard to gain buy in to the STC vision right from the start of the project, which had worked well.

The team performed excellently, despite a lot of other pressures from their day jobs because they had worked together, throughout the project, to understand what was mission-critical versus what could slip.

Jake

Jake Holder worked in an operational environment with both people and profit responsibilities, over a lengthy period. He was often called upon to lead small projects and had enjoyed them, so decided to move into project management when the opportunity presented itself.

He gained PRINCE2 accreditation along the way. He had gradually run larger and larger projects across most business areas and sectors. He was regarded as an experienced PM with a strong track record, with good commercial awareness, and strong people skills. He had previously run projects where the key resources were drawn from the business, but were not full time on the project.

The New Training Center

Employing 250 at the head office and 15,000 operational staff, NRB was a national retailer with 300 sites around the country. Historically, staff were trained locally in the regions, but it was thought more effective to bring it all together into a single training center, which was to become known as the STC. Large savings in external accommodation costs were expected as well as establishing a center of excellence to act as a showcase for the trainees.

The Facilities team got on with the project of organizing the physical build of the training center and hotel. This ran to schedule thanks, to the hard work of the Facilities team and their selection of an excellent prime contractor.

First Steps

At a routine monthly planning meeting, the CEO noticed the training center launch was due in six months, "Sally, what plans do you have to open this new facility?" he asked the operations director. "We've got six months to sort the fit out, business processes, recruit the team and so on."

"I'll get onto it," responded Sally.

"OK, Sally, this is a prestige launch. I don't need to remind you it's critical we have a smooth opening."

The STC was part of a strategic shift for NRB and so, the CEO had developed a clear documented vision for it. This described the purpose of the center as a driver for cultural change in the wider business, using the facility and its service as an exemplar for how to treat customers. It set out tangible requirements but, also, a series of words to describe the intangible elements. Everything about the STC was to be *premium* to reflect NRB's ambition for its customers, services, people, infrastructure, and so on. This went down to the coffee.

The Facilities team had used this for the main build and now Sally picked it up for the fit-out, organization, and processes.

"The senior management team has nodded around the board room table but now I need to make sure they're properly bought-in so I'll make sure they've all signed up to the vision, and the project brief I have prepared," responded Sally.

Setting up the Project

Sally Opsdee had been running the Operations Division for five years, knew the business well, and had plenty of experience making successful changes within her division. She had also been exposed to some tricky projects where many of the team had been directly from the business.

The next day, Sally met with Bob Bild, the Facilities Director. Sally and Bob had a good working relationship and often collaborated on projects.

"I need a PM to get us over the line and is a good stakeholder manager. By that, I mean someone that is sensitive to the operational demands our people face. I have seen the impact of assertive PMs who get the job done but leave a trail of human destruction behind them. I've heard good things about Jake."

"When it comes to delivery, he gets us over the line," agreed Bob. "He covers my back on audit, compliance and so on, but also has the nous to understand what needs to be pushed and when to back off from the people on the team. He understands the daily operational pressures in the business."

Satisfied, Sally pressed on, "I want to email out today, so we can crack on. I'll obviously go to their managers first, but what do you think of these other people for the team? I'm thinking Linda, Jim, Mo, Rashid, Sid and Jo?"

"I have established our project board and we have agreed with the business heads that we need their support and resources. This will be tough because there is pressure on operations right now. We have agreed the individuals. I appreciate they are the 'usual suspects', but to help they have been briefed by their managers and their objectives have been amended to take the project into account."

"We have also identified one of our training managers to be seconded on the project. This may be possible if we can free her up. She'll be able to work three days a week with the team and act as a 'super SME'."

"Yes, that's all the 'go-to' people. They're the experts," Bob replied.

A couple of days later, Sally met with Jake. "This is a great chance to show your prowess as a project manager. The CEO developed the STC vision and I've put together a brief outlining what we expect on opening." Smiling, she handed over a one-page brief. "We really want to wow the delegates and set an example for how things should be done. But we also want to make the best use of the skills and experience we have in the business without burning out the people. They will be challenged to balance their workload between BaU and the STC project."

Jake was really pleased to see the vision and the clear brief. The project board looked good and so too did the list of people on the team.

Planning the Project

Jake quickly organized a half-day workshop for the team to flesh out Sally's written brief. Enthusiasm for the new training center was high, and everyone turned up, keen to make an input.

Jake had arranged the workshop to start with a light lunch that gave him an opportunity to meet everyone. It also created a nice buzz because several of the project team members did not really know each other either.

"Thanks everyone for your attendance today," opened Jake. The first hour was dedicated to the STC vision. Jake had invited Malcom, the CEO, and Sally to spend that hour with the team to help embed the principles with them. Malcolm provided an impassioned explanation of the vision. "Thanks very much, Malcolm, that was great and will help us stay true to the vision," said Jake.

Malcolm left the workshop. "Sally has been working on this project for a short while and has produced a project brief that sets out the high-level components of the project. As you might expect, it stays true to the vision and provides the high-level structure for our project." Jake handed out the one-page copies. "We need your help today to turn that outline brief into a project plan and flush out risks, assumptions and dependencies."

"But before we start on that, I have reviewed the lessons learned from a previous large-scale project completed three years ago. I'd like to spend a few minutes running through that to see is there's anything we can learn as we detail out this project."

Jake expertly guided the project team through a product-based planning session, creating the product breakdown structure covering all the deliverables. The style was engaging, and Jake was able to keep the energy levels high, partly using humor and his self-deprecating style. He was able to balance seriousness and levity through the session. From this, the group were able to assess dependencies, identify assumptions, and document their risks and some headline mitigation.

To close the session, Jake helped the team clarify their involvement, ensure they understood the time commitment, and logged the challenges this posed with their day job.

Afterward, the team was chatting over a cup of tea.

Linda was impressed. "Well I'm impressed," she said. "The vision is great. The company is clearly serious and has invested time and money to get this right."

Rashid nodded agreement, "They seem to have thought about everything in detail which gives us a clear direction. We can use it as a benchmark for all of our decisions when we are designing the interiors, kitchen, processes and so on."

Linda continued, "Jake did well to get Malcolm and Sally to make some space in their busy diaries. I also liked the approach of starting from what we need for go live, then planning backwards. It could have been really dull, but Jake handled the session well and made it clear why we needed to do it."

Jim was less comfortable, "Do you realize how much work this will be. Sally's email didn't make that clear. Another project done as homework."

Rashid had worked with Jake before. "And Jake will make sure the project gets delivered so don't expect an easy ride. However, on the last project I was on, he worked with us on prioritizing between the needs of the project and our day jobs. There were times I had to miss some of the meetings, but the communication was so good, I didn't feel left out. Jake also followed up afterwards."

"I think we've seen that already—two-hour weekly review meetings plus one-hour one-to-ones have already gone into my diary. I hope he realizes I've got a full-time job," Jo's eyes turned skyward.

"Yes," said Mo, "and they run through with no gaps for month end."

Rashid responded, "I expect that is an oversight and I'm sure that if we speak to Jake, we can tweak the meeting schedule."

Jane chipped in, "My manager has already spoken to me about the project and we have agreed a revised set of objectives for me to the end of the year. That should help me, and she said it would be the same for every one of the project team."

Jake was aware of the team's concerns because he had run several projects where the project's resources were mostly drawn from the business. However, he had put in place what needed to be put in place so felt confident he could now build a plan, assign resources, and provide people with their task lists. Individual concerns could be picked up in the one-to-ones already booked.

Jake also wanted to make sure he had sign off from the business stakeholders so, once completed, he e-mailed a high-level "plan on a page," a detailed plan, and the initial risk log. The request was to review and sign off by the end of the week. However, Jake had cheekily booked 30-minute sessions in their diaries to enable a run through to cover off all the inevitable queries. He felt he needed to explain the key components of the plan, which was very detailed. He would use the sessions to gain *hearts and minds* and formal signoff.

He had his project board, his project team, a full set of diarized project meetings, his plan and signoff, so he could crack on! And, most important of all, he had a great vision with commitment from of all key stakeholders to see it through.

Jake had explained to Malcolm and Sally, "Strictly speaking the Project Board only approves the move from one stage to the next in a project. However, I have always found it essential to ensure the senior stakeholders are kept involved throughout, and so I generally cheat and extend the membership of the project board and diarize regular meetings. I will ensure each one has a clear agenda and purpose and I'll make sure they're short and punchy. It keeps everyone 'in the tent', if you see what I mean."

"I have also arranged weekly one-to-ones for us, Sally. This allows us to cover project matters 'offline' and for us to prep the other meetings. They're in your diary until beyond the end of the project."

"And finally, I have some templates for a fortnightly communication out to the rest of the business—an STC Newsletter if you like, to be slotted into the normal comms channels."

Running the Project

Fast forward six weeks and Jake was with Sally in their weekly meeting. "The plan has been a challenge, as we expected, Sally. By and large, we have hit our dates, but I have allowed some tasks to slip rather than push Mo and Jane too hard at this stage. They have had some difficult BaU issues crop up. We're on top of the plan so they were able to warn me in advance. A couple of the tasks weren't on the critical path, so I allowed them an extra week. A couple were but I was able to gain the support of other team members to get them reallocated." Sally nodded for him to continue. "At this stage, I will resist the temptation to be too assertive. It will wind up the project team and we need them for the long haul on this project. You'll need them in good shape afterwards too. We'll retain their support this way. I also make sure the difficult conversations on deadlines happen in the weekly one-to-ones and not in the team meetings."

Sally was concerned. "This doesn't sound like a 'green' project, Jake. I don't want to scare the senior guys, but we do need to get on top of this."

"I agree", said Jake. "I propose we set the project to amber. We have a number of issues, but we have a plan to ensure we still hit the overall deadline."

He continued, "There's no point pretending. I've seen projects that go 'green, green, green, train crash'. If we're honest on status, we get trusted and support when we need it. I am all over the plan's start dates. In my experience, there is a tendency, for understandable reasons, in operational environments, for people to just do the 'urgent and important' tasks. Or only start when their trousers are on fire! This causes problems for those dependent on their work."

Sally leaned forward in her chair, "Well, Jake, I appreciate your candor. This project is just as important as anything else in the business right now. I'll back you up."

"There is something you can do, please. I must gently remind people of meeting and report dates. We can miss the odd report, but I do want people at the meetings because it's the most efficient method of comms and knowledge sharing. Any chance you could attend the next project meeting for a few minutes and deliver a 'thanks so far' and an upbeat pep talk?"

"On my side, I'll help with some of the practicalities, for example, using dial in as an option for the meetings. We can also tweak some of the days and times where necessary. They will always happen weekly—I'm not compromising on that."

Back on Track, Sort Of

At the 12-week meeting with Sally, Jake was able to report the plan was just about back on track. "As you would expect, I have sought feedback from my peers across the business about impacts on BaU," Sally told Jake. "There have been stresses and strains but since they all understand the importance of what we are doing, I didn't get my head bitten off. And they are not backward in coming forward so I'm taking comfort from that."

"We're not out of the woods yet though. We need to re-locate five outlets and it will require Rashid and Jim to plan out the move, so they will be under pressure to that, this and their day job," said Sally.

"OK, I understand and thanks for the tip off. I'll review the plan myself, then run through what can be reallocated or slipped with Rashid and Jim, and the rest of the team. I'll come back to you with resource and budget requirements if we can't resolve ourselves," Jake responded.

"With the greatest respect to the project team, we must ensure the business decides the priorities between the projects and BaU. We must also ensure the project team doesn't become frazzled because this won't help any of us."

"I'll need your support with the Project Board because I predict the likely outcome of the plan review will be that we need complete the STC office fit out beyond the opening date. It's back of house so won't affect the delegate experience but will give us the breathing space we need for Jim's work on the other project," said Jake.

"Agreed. Let's go to the Project Board early with this. We can re-jig the move in plan for the STC Admin Team," responded Sally.

Jake, with Sally's unwavering support, had maintained team spirit, and Jake had fought to keep in the budget enough funds for a pre-go-live jolly for the team. This went down well and was good preparation for the usual stresses and strains of a go-live.

The business was fully briefed on the go-live plan and provided support for the *unknown, unknowns* that inevitably occur in an operation of this nature on Day One.

Many around the business had been asking Jake about the opening date. "1st September," said Jake. "Yeah, right—but when is it really opening?" was the most common retort.

Opening Day

Opening day arrived and the facility was in good shape. The front of house looked fantastic, and the arrival processes worked a treat. This was borne out by the subsequent delegate experience survey, which was one of the best NRB had ever had.

The less said about the state of the admin office, the better. However, that was hidden, and the admin team were able to work remotely for the next couple of weeks while it was finished.

The budget was five percent overspent, but still within expectations of the business.

The project team met for a *day one* review late afternoon. "Every good project delivery needs cakes and here they are," said Jake as he unveiled a sugar-laden feast. "Well done, Jake," whispered Sally. "The smiles on the faces of these guys tells me everything I need to know about this project. We got the project over the line with both the business and the people in good shape."

"Thanks, Sally. In my experience, it is rare you are remembered for small delays, reduced scope and a bit of overspend. You do get remembered if the final output doesn't work, or you've ruined the people on the project. I try to keep that in mind on everything I do."

Meeting the CEO

Standing outside the CEO's office, Jake paused before knocking the door. He was nervous as he knew the project had not been perfect.

Despite Jake's confidence on the opening day, and Sally's support, the facts were that the project delivered part of the scope late and it was over budget. There had been a strain on BaU and the project team. Jake was not quite sure how this would play out with the CEO.

Malcom greeted him with a broad smile, "Thank you, Jake, for delivering the STC vision," he beamed. "To be honest, I knew this was a tall order when we started but Sally, you and the project team have done a great job."

Glossary

As-homework staff	Staff with BaU responsibilities working part time on the project
APM	Association for Project Management
BaU	Business as usual
Composite project	Projects resourced with a blend of staff dedicated to the project and as-homework staff
Day job/real work	BaU responsibilities of as-homework staff against which they are evaluated
Homework	Work done above the normal BaU schedule and, often, outside normal working hours
PM	Project manager
PMI	Project Management Institute
PMO	Project management office
PRINCE2	A structured project management method
RAID	A log for Risks, Actions, Issues, and Decisions
SME	Subject matter expert

About the Authors

Stuart Copeland BSc (Hons), MCMI, MBCS

Stuart is a UK-based business consultant, specializing in the leadership of change projects with significant complexity, criticality, and scale. He has run over 100 projects, across multiple sectors and with large and small organizations. He is a graduate of Cardiff University and a member of the Chartered Management Institute, the Institute of Interim Management, and the British Computer Society. He is PRINCE2 and MSP accredited. Prior to setting up an independent consultancy, he held a range of general management and business improvement positions in a large automotive group. Throughout his working life, he has seen the importance of looking after those who support projects to ensure they can successfully manage their day job, their project, and their own well-being.

Andy Coaton CFA, CEng, MBA, BSc(Hons), DipM

Andy is a UK-based business consultant and visiting lecturer on two post-graduate programs at the University of London. He has many years of professional experience scoping and defining, and then managing numerous engineering and consultancy projects introducing change for international corporates through to startups. He holds the designation of Chartered Engineer and Chartered Financial Analyst and holds a master's degree in Business Administration from Cranfield School of Management. He was seven years with PricewaterhouseCoopers (PwC), including leading the Emergent Technology Team in London.

Index

Alphabets 'f' and 't' after page numbers indicate figure and table respectively.

OTHER TITLES IN THE PORTFOLIO AND PROJECT MANAGEMENT COLLECTION

Timothy J. Kloppenborg, Xavier University, Editors

- *Core Concepts of Project Management* by David L. Olson
- *Capital Project Management, Volume III* by Robert N. McGrath
- *Capital Project Management, Volume II* by Robert N. McGrath
- *Capital Project Management, Volume I* by Robert N. McGrath
- *Executing Global Projects* by James Marion
- *Project Communication from Start to Finish* by Geraldine E. Hynes
- *The Lost Art of Planning Projects* by Louise Worsley
- *Project Portfolio Management, Second Edition* by Clive N. Enoch
- *Adaptive Project Planning* by Louise Worsley
- *Passion, Persistence, and Patience* by Alfonso Bucero

Announcing the Business Expert Press Digital Library

Concise e-books business students need for classroom and research

This book can also be purchased in an e-book collection by your library as

- a one-time purchase,
- that is owned forever,
- allows for simultaneous readers,
- has no restrictions on printing, and
- can be downloaded as PDFs from within the library community.

Our digital library collections are a great solution to beat the rising cost of textbooks. E-books can be loaded into their course management systems or onto students' e-book readers.
The **Business Expert Press** digital libraries are very affordable, with no obligation to buy in future years. For more information, please visit **www.businessexpertpress.com/librarians**. To set up a trial in the United States, please email **sales@businessexpertpress.com**.

www.ingramcontent.com/pod-product-compliance
Lightning Source LLC
Chambersburg PA
CBHW061325220326
41599CB00026B/5042